CISTERCIAN STUDIES SERIES: NUMBER ONE HUNDRED-EIGHT

# THE LIFE OF SAINT MARY MAGDALENE
## AND OF HER SISTER SAINT MARTHA

D0815015

CISTERCIAN STUDIES SERIES: NUMBER ONE HUNDRED-EIGHT

# The Life of Saint Mary Magdalene and of her Sister Saint Martha

A Medieval Biography
Translated and Annotated by
David Mycoff

Cistercian Publications
Kalamazoo
1989

This translation is based on the latin edition by
Etienne-Michel Faillon (1848),
reprinted in J.-P. Migne, Patrologia Latina 112:1431-1508.

Available from
Cistercian Publications
Saint Joseph's Abbey
Spencer, MA 01562

The work of Cistercian Publications is made possible in part by
support from Western Michigan University to
The Institute of Cistercian Studies.

**Library of Congress Cataloguing-in-Publication Data:**

Rabanus Maurus, Archbishop of Mainz, 784?-856.
[De vita Beatae Mariae Magdalenae et sororis ejus Sanctae
Marthae. English]
Saint Mary Magdalene and her sister Saint Martha:
a twelfth-century biography/translated, with commentary
and introduction, by David Mycoff.
p. cm.—(Cistercian studies series; no. 108)
Translation of: De vita Beatae Mariae Magdalenae et sororis
ejus Sanctae Marthae/Rabanus Maurus, Archbishop of Mainz.
Bibliography:p.
1. Mary Magdalene, Saint. 2. Martha, Saint. 3. Christian
saints-Biography–Early works to 1800. 4. Bible. N.T.–Biography–Early works to 1800. I. Mycoff, David A., 1953-
II. Title. III. Series
BS2485.R3313 1989
226'.092'2–dc19
[B]

88-37494
CIP

*Printed in the United States of America*

# ACKNOWLEDGMENTS

The colleagues, teachers, and friends who helped me in various ways at various places during my work on this project are too numerous to mention in these brief acknowledgments. My chief debt, here as elsewhere, is to Professor James P. Carley, who directed the dissertation of which this translation is a part and who saw me through the rigors of graduate school with patience, humor, and insight. I also want to thank Professors Russell Peck and Thomas Hahn for their useful criticism and timely encouragement. Dr E. Rozanne Elder, editorial director of Cistercian Publications, has been an ever-patient and helpful editor.

The West Virginia Institute of Technology provided travel funds which made it possible for me to work on revisions of this material during the summer of 1985. Professor Peck and the University of Rochester's Medieval House extended their hospitality during that summer. Warren Wilson College provided funds to assist my research during the summers of 1987 and 1988.

FOR MEI

# CONTENTS

# INTRODUCTION

W hen in April of 1518 the great humanist Jacques Lefèvre d'Étaples published his *De Marie Magdalena,* a treatise attacking the Latin Church's traditional identification of Mary Magdalene, Mary of Bethany, and the penitent woman of Luke 7: 36-50, neither ecclesiastical authority nor the church at large was prepared to accept such a radical disruption of exegesis and piety.[1] Within three years, some fifteen major treatises — including three by another remarkable humanist scholar, John Fisher, Bishop of Rochester — had been written in connection with the controversy Lefèvre initiated. Lefèvre himself had been censured by the theological faculty of the Sorbonne and his works placed on the index.[2] The passions of the controversialists were fueled by wider issues of theological perspective and method, liturgical precedent, and cultic observance, and behind these lay a millenium of tradition.[3] Although the Eastern Church from an early date had maintained that the two Marys and the nameless penitent were separate, the West, even before the time of Gregory the Great, who provided an authoritative sanction for the view in his *Homilies,*[4] identified them as one, and in an effort to maintain harmony between the various pertinent scriptural passages, constructed a coherent life story for this single Magdalen.[5] This story became a primary source of images and archetypal patterns for reflection on the Church's understanding of two fundamental matters: the right relations between the active and contemplative lives and the process by which penitent sinners are reconciled to God and thereby freed for growth in the spiritual life.[6] Just as Mary Magdalene, representing the contemplative life, and Martha, representing the active life, are two separate persons with clearly defined vocations which limit their proper activities,

1

so all contemplative and active persons possess distinct vocations subject to the defining limits of those vocations. Just as Mary's vocation is designated as 'better' than Martha's, so the contemplative vocation is higher than the active. Just as Mary and Martha, as sisters, should live in sisterly love, recognizing the different dignities of their callings but holding each other in respect and affection, so should followers of the contemplative and active lives acknowledge the distinctions but live in mutual esteem and charity. And just as that dreadful sinner, Mary Magdalene, through penitence becomes the special servant and friend of Christ, so should all penitents have faith in the efficacy of God's absolution and mercy.

There was, then, in the life of the one Mary Magdalene—sinner, penitent, and contemplative—something to appeal to practically every order of medieval society; something that spoke to the hopes, anxieties, and aspirations of nearly everyone. Monastics could find in the story of the contemplative Mary a language, imagery, and pattern by which to interpret their experience and concerns; laics in the world could discover in the repentant and forgiven Magdalen hope for deliverance from the moral ambiguities of their lives. It is little wonder, therefore, that by the eleventh century the cult of the Magdalen was universally popular in the West, or that —despite a decline in the later fourteenth and fifteenth centuries—an attack on established Magdalen traditions in the early sixteenth century could generate a controversy of seriousness and acrimony. At work were not merely the inertia of tradition and the recalcitrance of authority, but the forces that defend the perspectives by which people understand some of the most important dimensions of their lives. So deeply did the old legend speak, and so strong was the resistance to abandoning the particular self-understanding that it affirmed, that despite an increasingly impressive body of critical-textual argument to the contrary, the tradition had serious defenders until after the end of the nineteenth century. Today, however, both

Roman Catholicism and Protestantism agree with Eastern Orthodoxy in distinguishing between Mary Magdalene, Mary of Bethany, and the penitent in Luke.

Many different texts related to each other by very complicated lines of transmission were brought together to form the legend of Mary Magdalene known to the high Middle Ages. Even a basic outline of the legend's development will be clearer if a summary of the story in its fully-developed and relatively stable thirteenth-century form, as told by Jacobus de Voragine in *Legenda aurea* (probably not later than 1267), is first provided.

Mary Magdalene, the legend goes, was born of noble parents, the decendants of kings. With her sister Martha and brother Lazarus she possessed Magdalo, Bethany, and a great part of the city of Jersualem. But, succumbing to the temptations of riches, beauty, and youth, she forsook her heritage and became a common sinner until at length, inspired by the Holy Spirit, she came to the house of Simon the Leper, the Pharisee of Bethany, where Christ was dining, and having bathed his feet with her penitential tears, dried them with her hair, and anointed them with precious ointment, she received Christ's absolution, despite the murmurings of the Pharisee. Christ delivered her from seven demons (sins), and made her his particular friend and servant, for she provided for the material needs of Christ and his disciples on their journeys. He defended her against her sister's complaints and raised her brother Lazarus from the dead for her sake. Mary again anointed Christ soon before his passion, and stood near the cross, and brought ointment to the tomb on Easter morning. She was the first to whom the Risen Christ appeared, and she received from him the commission to announce his resurrection to the apostles. For this she is designated apostle to the apostles.

Fourteen years after Christ's ascension, during a great persecution in Jerusalem, Mary Magdalene, Martha, Lazarus, Saint Maximin, and other Christians were put to sea in a rudderless boat by the unbelievers. By the providence of God they arrived safely in Marseilles, where they sheltered under the portico of a pagan temple. Seeing the people come to sacrifice to the idols, Mary Magdalene preached the Gospel to them and converted them. Shortly afterwards, she also converted the prince of the region and his wife by obtaining the favor of the conception of a son and heir for them, but not without first having to appear three times to them in a vision, threatening them with punishment for their sumptuous living and neglect of God's poor. The prince, wishing to test the truth of Mary's doctrine, resolved to journey to Rome to see Saint Peter. Against his wishes, his pregnant wife decided to accompany him. The couple left their possessions in the care of Mary Magdalene, and having received her blessing, set to ship.

Soon there arose a terrible storm, during which the wife was delivered of a son and died. The sailors superstitiously wanted to cast her body overboard, but the prince prevailed on them to abandon the body and the living infant on a forsaken rock in the sea. Commending his dear ones to Mary Magdalene and to God, the prince completed his journey to Rome, was received by Peter, and undertook with him a pilgrimage to the Holy Land. Confirmed in his faith and having completed his pilgrimage, the prince set out on the return voyage to Marseilles.

Along the way, the ship happened by the rock where the wife and child had been left, so the prince had the sailors set in there. They found the child still alive. More marvelously, as the prince offered thanksgiving to Mary Magdalene, the body of the wife also came to life. The wife declared that while the prince had been visiting the Holy Land with Saint Peter, she had also been there with Mary Magdalene, who had preserved the lives of herself and the child. Rejoicing, the family completed the voyage to Marseilles, where they found Mary Magdalene preaching to her disciples. After receiving baptism, the noble couple assisted in completing the conversion of the land.

Meanwhile, Mary Magdalene, 'desirous of sovereign

contemplation', sought out a desert place and remained there in solitude for thirty years. Each day, at each canonical hour, she was lifted up into the heavenly choirs and fed on celestial food. One day a priest who had also found solitude nearby, saw her elevation, and wondering at the occurrence, approached. The holiness of the place hindered his movement, but at last he spoke with the saint, who told him her story and commanded him to go to Saint Maximin, her spiritual adviser in earlier days, and tell him that she would appear amid angels in his oratory on the day after Easter. The priest did as he was told, and all happened as Mary Magdalene had said. She appeared to Maximin, spoke with him, received communion from him, and then died. Maximin buried her honorably. Jacobus completes his narrative with a second, slightly different account of the Magdalen's years in solitude, to which he adds a selection of short accounts of miracles she performed after her death and a narration of how her relics were conveyed from the abbey of Saint Maximin to the abbey of Vézelay.

There are, then, five parts to this fully-developed Magdalen legend: the pre-ascension life; the story of the voyage to Marseilles; the story of the prince of Marseilles; the account of the thirty-year solitude, death, and burial; and the post-burial miracles and translation of relics. The pre-ascension life is the product of the patristic harmonizing of scattered scriptural passages which, in the view of the medieval Western Church, all pertained to Mary Magdalene. The earliest extant text that assembles these patristic motifs into a single, concise, coherent narrative appears to be a tenth-century sermon on the Magdalen attributed to Saint Odo of Cluny (BHL 5439).[7] Close in date is a legend, titled by the prominent scholar of the Magdalen legend and cult, Victor Saxer, *Vita apostolica Mariae Magdalenae*,[8] which tells of the Magdalen's voyage to Marseilles and her career in Gaul, omitting the stories of the prince of Marseilles and the thirty year seclusion. The remote source of the account of Mary's solitude is the legend of Mary of Egypt, first told in the *Life of Cyriacus* by Cyril of Scythopolis.[9] By the ninth century, the Egyptian's story had been adapted for Mary Magdalene in a piece titled by Saxer, *Vita eremitica Mariae Magdalenae* (BHL 5453-5456).[10] The *Vita apostolica* and *Vita eremitica* were conflated into a single piece to form *Vita apostolico-eremitica* (BHL 5443-5448),[11] apparently in the eleventh century during the resurgence of Western eremiticism that began in northern Italy. Another composite piece, *Vita evangelico-apostolica* (BHL 5450)[12] assembles the pre-ascension material of Odo's sermon with the post-ascension material of *Vita apostolico-eremitca*, abbreviating the account of the contemplative retreat. The prince of Marseilles story is brought in by the *vita, Postquam Dominus N.I.C.* (BHL 5457),[13] perhaps a collaboration of sorts between hagiographers and provençal romance-writers. The miracle accounts are selected by Jacobus from the wealth of such stories that accumulated over the years, some of which, of course, were adopted from the miracle stories of other saints. The translation account — which figured so importantly in the controversies between the abbey of Saint Maximin and the abbey of Vézelay regarding the possession of the Magdalen's relics — are recorded in pieces designated as *Translationis narratio prior* (BHL 5442, 5488) and *Translationis narratio posterior* (BHL 5489-5492).[14]

Between the ninth and eleventh centuries, then, a process of conflation and assimilation established the essential contours of the legend Jacobus relates. Other texts, from the twelfth and early thirteenth centuries, not significant enough to mention in this short survey, added details or settled in a relatively definitive way matters treated inconsistently before. After Jacobus, most hagiographers — working in both Latin and the vernaculars — follow his version or a version derived from it. The piece translated here (abbrev. VBMM) is a bit earlier than *Legenda aurea,* but the main outlines of the legend were established by the time it was written. The omission of the prince of Marseilles story, the skepticism regarding the popular story of the Magdalen's eremitic retreat, and the neglect of the translation accounts are therefore almost certainly the result of choice rather than of ignorance regarding the traditions in question. The problem raised by the omission of miracle stories will be treated later in this introduction. The *vita* itself gives the author's reason for doubting the eremitic life (ll. 2051-2077). He objects to the falsity of ascribing the story to Josephus and he dislikes the literalizing of things that should be understood in a spiritual sense. And although the movement of mature cenobites to an eremitic life is sanctioned by the benedictine Rule as interpreted at the time, the notion that even a very great saint might obtain the perfection of contemplation while living in the flesh may have offended the author's sense of right doctrine and realism. Regarding the translation accounts, one can only speculate about what political affiliations, loyalties, or tastes the omission might imply.

## AUTHORSHIP AND DATE

Although Migne included VBMM among the works of the carolingian exegete, Rabanus Maurus, evidence for this attribution rests chiefly on the poor testimony of a single late manuscript, Oxford, Magdalen College, MS 89 (*c.* 1408), which bears the title, *Rabanus de Vita Mariae Magdalenae,* and on Étienne-Michel Faillon's attempt in the mid-nineteenth century to demonstrate Rabanus' authorship by citing parallels between the exegete's works and VBMM. Scholars as early as William Cave, *Scriptorum Ecclesiasticorum Historia Literaria* (1688; 1698), had noted the manuscript's attribution, but nobody before Faillon mentioned it without reservation. Although Faillon has had supporters, the balance of opinion almost from the date of his publication has been against him, and critics have included scholars of such authority as the Bollandists, Paul Meyer, and Henri Leclercq.[15] While there is now general agreement that Rabanus was *not* the author, a viable alternative attribution has yet to be found. Indeed, so great are the problems of creating a case for attribution that few have ventured a suggestion. D'Ozouville argued that the *vita* was a fifteenth-century forgery, but the existence of manuscripts manifestly written before that time disposes of this suggestion. More recently, Saxer has made an interesting if not unassailable case for cistercian authorship.[16]

Saxer's most convincing evidence is bibliographic. Of the seven known manuscripts containing VBMM, one dates from the later twelfth century, two from the thirteenth, one from the fourteenth, two from the fifteenth century, and one is undated by Saxer.[17] The earliest manuscript, Montpellier, Faculté de Mèdecine, MS I. vol. 3, is from Clairvaux. Another early manuscript, Troyes, Bibliothèque Municipale, MS 444, bears the inscriptions *ex libris de Clairvaux* and *Liber sancte Marie Clareuallis* on fol. 129[r]. This manuscript also contains works by Geoffrey of Auxerre, Bernard's one-time secretary and abbot of several different cistercian abbeys at different times. MS BL Arundel 63 binds VBMM with the works of the english Cistercian, Aelred of Rievaulx and with Saint Bernard's life of Saint Malachy the Irishman. MS BL Add. 24641 binds VBMM with meditations ascribed to Bernard and with Bernard's *Apology to Abbot William*. Inscriptions on fol. 114[v] of this manuscript show that it was owned by a franciscan foundation.[18] Although such evidence cannot conclusively demonstrate cistercian authorship, it does establish that Cistercians or those greatly influenced by cistercian spirituality (the Franciscans) played the major role in preserving and transmitting the work, that they were its primary audience, and that they considered it worthy of being included along with some of the masterpieces of cistercian spiritual writing.

Saxer's other line of argument, perhaps less rigorous but very suggestive, proceeds by citing instances of characteristically bernardine vocabulary and imagery in VBMM. The most impressive parallel is one Faillon used to try to show VBMM's influence on Bernard, though chronology shows the influence must have worked in the other direction.

| *Bernard:* | *VBMM:* |
|---|---|
| Et forte provide ob hoc Dominus Iesus paratam sibi confectionem expendi noluit in suo corpore mortuo, ut servaret vivo. Vivit enim Ecclesia, quae manducat panem vivum, que de caelo descendit. Ipsa est carius corpus Christi, quod ne mortem gustaret, morti illud alterum traditum fuisse nullus christianus ignorat. [SBOp 1: 64-65.] | Noluit ea expendi, Filius Dei, in suo corpore mortuo, ut servaret vivo. Vivit enim Ecclesia Dei, quae manducat panem vivum. Ipsa est charius corpus Christi, quod ne moriatur, morti illud alterum traditum est. [PL 112: 1480.] |

Because of Bernard's widespread and lasting influence, such parallels cannot, however, convincingly demonstrate cistercian authorship. Yet they do show, as Saxer suggests, that VBMM is 'stamped with the spiritual doctrine of St Bernard', and that the piece was almost certainly 'composed in a milieu pervaded by the spiritual teaching of the mystical doctor'.[19] The commentary presented with the present translation aims primarily at elucidating the pervasive bernardine spirituality of the work, and also tries to suggest some of the ways the primary audience might have read it. Since, unless otherwise stated, the notes do not identify immediate sources but rather do suggest a line of interpretation, I sometimes cite works which may indeed be of later date than the VBMM.

Unless further evidence regarding authorship and date can be found, then, only a generalized attribution can confidently be made: the *vita* was composed in the late twelfth century by an anonymous compiler deeply influenced by the spirituality of Saint Bernard.

SOURCES

I have not attempted an exhaustive study of the sources of VBMM, partly because some of the probable sources are inedited and not readily accessible and partly because the task of unravelling the tangled lines of transmission from remote sources through intermediary sources — however valuable such a study might be for its own sake or for what it might reveal about the transmission of medieval texts generally — is not likely to contribute much to an understanding of VBMM itself. The discussion below is therefore only a general outline.[20]

VBMM, like much medieval hagiography, is a composite work. Among its chief sources are the Bible, which is quoted or paraphrased extensively; the *Vita apostolica Mariae Magdalenae*, perhaps through extracts contained in the lections of many breviaries for the feast of Saint Mary Magdalene, the sermon on the Magdalen attributed to Saint Odo of Cluny, possibly through the *Vita apostolica* or an intermediary of that text; Eusebius' *Ecclesiastical History*, almost certainly through an intermediary; and Saint Augustine's *In Johannis Evangelium Tractatus CXXIV* — perhaps through works whose texts for relevant passages are virtually indistinguishable from Augustine's: Bede, *In S. Joannis Evangelium Expositio;* Alcuin, *Commentaria in S. Joannis Evangelium;* and Rabanus, *Homiliae in Evangelia et Epistolas.* To this list I would also add, as a likely source, a *Vita Marthae* composed by pseudo-Marcella (BHL 5545-5546) which is a source used by Vincent of Beauvais in *Speculum historiale* and probably accounts for the scattered verbal parallels and other correspondences between VBMM and Vincent's work. There should also be recognized a generalized 'patristic exegetical tradition', for VBMM is full of *topoi* and glosses found so often in pre-scholastic exegesis that no precise source can be defined for them. And there is, finally, the bernardine influence, sometimes found in close verbal correspondences and sometimes more generalized, but always present.

The *vita's* author makes varied use of his sources. At times he borrows almost *verbatim*, as in the passage from Saint Bernard quoted above. Usually, however, his appropriation is more free. A typical hagiographer in this matter, he abbreviates, amplifies, paraphrases, or transports passages from one kind of context to a radically different one. A characteristic passage appears in ll. 1361-1372. The author attempts to explain why Mary Magdalene, in the harmonized account of Easter morning, returns a second time to the tomb after hearing the angel announce the resurrection earlier:

> Nevertheless — not believing in what she herself had seen before daylight: the empty tomb; the apostle with whom she had sought him; the apostles to whom she had been sent to tell the news; the women who accompanied her, who had so often been frustrated in their search for him; the angels from whom she had heard that he was not there but risen — she bent down, weeping, and peered into the tomb, moved and inspired by the one she sought, who inflamed her soul with the fire of love and who guided her in not believing easily in the apostles, or the women, or even in her own eyes.

The author has developed this elegant if prolix explanation

on a hint provided by two scant sentences in Augustine's
*In Johannis Evangelium Tractatus CXXIV* (121.1; CC 36:
664):

> Was it that her grief was so excessive that she hardly
> thought she could believe either their eyes or her
> own? Or was it rather by some divine impulse that
> her mind led her to look within?[21]

The brief suggestion that Augustine makes regarding the
possible activity of the Spirit gives the author occasion to bring
in one of his favorite themes — the action of prevenient grace,
thereby permitting him to impose a little thematic unity as
well.

A different kind of adaptation, illustrating the author's
most inventive use of sources, occurs at ll. 1869-1878. Here the
author wishes to explain Mary's grief and feeling of forsaken-
ness after Christ's ascension, emotions which, by clear implication, are analogous to the contemplative's experience of
spiritual dryness — absence of the presence of Christ. The
author closely paraphrases part of the famous lament for
Gerard of Clairvaux delivered by Saint Bernard in Sermon 26 of
his series on the canticle. The verbal similarities in the english
translations are found also in the latin versions:

| *Bernard:* | *VBMM:* |
|---|---|
| It is but human and necessary that we respond to our friends with feeling: that we be happy in their company, disappointed in their absence. Social intercourse especially be- tween friends, cannot | Truly, amid such great glorifications of Christ, Mary Magdalene out- wardly rejoiced with an in- effable joy in the glory of her Lord and Redeemer, but inwardly she grieved with the grief of a forsaken |

| *Bernard: (Cont.)* | *VBMM: (Cont.)* |
|---|---|
| be purposeless; the reluctance to part and the yearning for each other when separated, indicate how meaningful their mutual love must be when they are together. [CF 7: 69; SBOp 1: 178.] | lover for his corporal absence. It is natural, I say, very natural, and even necessary, that fast friends be happy and joyful when together and tearful and sad when apart. The greatness of love for the one departed is measured by the tears of the one remaining behind; the love felt in the presence of the beloved equals the sorrow felt at parting. |

The allusiveness—few of the *vita's* readers would miss the appropriation of Bernard—and shift of context link at least four different affections here, underlining their similarities and analogies, suggesting how they can be used as means to understand things that from a different perspective are quite alien to each other. Two particular affections—Bernard's for his brother Gerard and Mary Magdalene's for Jesus—are paralleled; both together are paralleled to a general human affection for friends; and all are paralleled to the spiritual person's love for God. The passage is a good example of the workings of a sensibility shaped by a spiritual teaching that affirms the theological relevance of human relations. All the more extended examples of indebtedness to a particular source demonstrate the operation of this kind of sensibility. Whatever the text he reads, the author sees it through the lenses of his bernardine preoccupations, a perspective which often produces notable originality even when at first glance the material seems to have been lifted *verbatim*. Perhaps more than anything else, the integrity, the wholeness, of the author's spiritual perspective prevents his composite work from seeming as disjointed as composites often are. Despite its many partitions of the narrative, its frequent interpretative digressions, its not always graceful jumping back and forth from the story of Mary to the story of Martha, its often awkward transitions, and its rather perfunctory ending, VBMM maintains a unity of tone, style, and theme that derives as much from the author's vision as from his skill in twelfth-century rhetoric.

### SOME PURPOSES, PREOCCUPATIONS, AND THEMES

The aim and intention of all speech, for an observant medieval monk, should be charity. The role of a story-teller — of a hagiographer — and of the story he tells is to help set in motion a process by which the audience is moved to love first a person or other entity worthy of love and then, through that love, to love God more fully and more fruitfully. For the author of VBMM, these intentions translate into stirring the reader's love and admiration of Mary Magdalene to such a degree that the reader follows her course of life and himself attains to the happiness of contemplative love. As one extended summary passage in praise of the Magdalen (ll. 1736-1748) says:

> Happy is the one who has heard all this concerning Mary Magdalene with pleasure. More happy the one who has believed it and rememberd it with devotion. Yet more happy the one who has marveled at Mary's holiness, and reverenced her with love, and burned to imitate her. And most happy by far the one who has been so moved by and who has taken such delight in the surpassing fragrance of Mary's deeds that he has followed the example of

her conversion, has imprinted in himself the image
of her repentance, and has filled his spirit with her
devotion, to the degree that he has made himself a
partaker of that best part which she chose.

Informing this encomium and the aims it implies is a
typological pattern of ascent from lesser forms of virtue to the
highest form in which one becomes a kind of 'god' and a
perfect 'likeness' to God. The operative force in this process is
love. The reader, it is implied, has been made to love the
Magdalen (who has passed through all three stages of ascent)
so greatly that he identifies completely with her, so much so
that her 'image' becomes stamped in his soul. In the author's
words, the reader of the story of the Magdalen passes through
'pleasure' to 'reverence', 'love', and a 'burning desire' to imitate her, to active imitation and identification with her. The
three stages of ascent are echoed in three stages of affection,
and these in turn correspond to three degrees of 'happiness',
the last of which the passage quoted above addresses.

If love is the force that powers such transformation, the
source of love is grace. It is not surprising, then, that one of the
central preoccupations of VBMM is what theologians would
call the mystery of prevenient and indwelling grace. A few examples help illustrate this recurrent theme.

Chapter VI describes Mary Magdalene's first encounter with
Christ. The Magdalen has reached the nadir of moral depravity
and begun to despise herself, but news of a merciful prophet
whom some believe to be the Messiah fills her with hope and she
resolves to go to him as he dines with a Pharisee who lives in her
town. When she enters the dinner chamber, the prophet, Jesus,
receives her at once, for, as the author pointedly remarks, he had
indeed come to her first in the Spirit:

Groaning within her heart and conscience over
these things [her sin and loss], she went to the feast,

where it was said the Son of God was in attendance. Nor did she escape the notice of the one to whom she had come, and from whom no secrets are hidden; for in truth, he came to her first, through the sevenfold gifts of the Spirit, bringing to her the sweetness of his blessing, drawing her to himself, hastening her on her way. (ll. 217-224.)

In this archetypal account of conversion and forgiveness, divine grace precedes human action. Before Mary can turn back to God and seek his forgiveness, God must come to her. Grace is prevenient: it comes before all human efforts to acquire it, even before the repentance that might seem to be a condition for receiving grace. Yet divine initiative does not deprive human choices and the actions issuing from those choices of reality. Later in VBMM, in a passage defending the right of human priests to forgive sins in the name of God, the author remarks: 'What man does through God, God truly does, and—what is better and of greater truth—what God does through man, man truly does' (ll. 796-798). No neat separation of divine initiative and human response is allowed here. The theology informing VBMM reconciles what at first seems to be mutually exclusive: the reality of divine omnipotence and the reality of human freedom and action. The apparent paradox that divine and human actions are distinct but not separate is overcome by emphasis on the indwelling character of grace. Grace is not added or attached externally to a person. It is not an ornament or garment, things in which a person can be vested but which are not really a part of the person. Rather, grace enters a person and transfigures him from within. Since it comes from God but dwells within a human being, it fully incorporates both the divine and the human. The VBMM uses language of impregnation, conception, and birth to express this notion of grace. The conversion passage quoted above continues:

Impregnated with these [the seven gifts of the
Spirit], by faith she conceived a good hope within
herself and gave birth to a fervent charity. Her gift
to the Savior, the alabaster vessel, was an outward
sign of those blessed inner motions and of the
burning fire of her contrition. With a conscience
fruitfully laden with these things and with the
fullness of her repentance for her past life, teeming
with a devotion pleasing to God, which stirred
within her a certain hope of pardon, she came to
the supper of the lord. (ll. 227-236).

The repentant Magdalen in this passage is pictured as a woman
in the late stages of pregnancy; her soul is a fruitful womb
teeming with spiritual gifts. The image is repeated in other
contexts which suggest many affinities between Mary the
Mother of God and the 'pregnant' Mary Magdalene. Indeed,
the 'mother' image is extended to every believer in whom the
mystery of indwelling grace operates. For example, the VBMM
glosses Christ's words, 'Whoever does the will of my Father is
my brother, and my sister, and my mother' as follows:

He gives birth to me who, hearing me in his heart,
preaches me; he becomes my mother, whose voice
engenders the love of me in others. (ll. 474-477)

The thought is developed in the account of the woman who
blessed the Virgin's womb and breasts. I quote at length to in-
clude all of the extended metaphor:

There was present at that place, along with other
religious women who ministered to the Saviour,
Marcella, of whom we spoke before, the follower
and procuress of the blessed Martha, a woman of
great devotion and faith. Believing in the Incarnate
Saviour with wonderful sincerity, trust, and confidence, she confounded the chief priests and

Pharisees by raising her voice above the crowd and crying aloud to the Saviour: 'Blessed is the womb that bore you, the woman who gave you out of her flesh the seed that formed the substance of your body; and blessed are the breasts that gave you suck, the woman whose flesh was the source of that milk which nourished your flesh!' To which the Saviour said: 'Not only is that mother blessed, who, as you say, engendered with her flesh and fed with her milk the one who is the Word of God; but also blessed are they who, hearing my word, conceive the Word of God in the womb of their souls. They rejoice in the same gift of grace if, having received the seed of the Word by faith, they keep it and nourish it with the breasts of hope and charity.' (ll. 479-499.)

This passage considerably expands the Vulgate version, in which the woman says only: 'Blessed be the womb that bore you and the breasts that gave you suck.' The additions the author of VBMM makes suggest that he wanted to emphasize the closeness of the tie between Christ and his mother and the fact that Christ's body grows out of the very substance of his mother's body. For the mystical interpretation of the passage, this unrestrained incarnationalism has important implications. The material or phenomenal reality of Christ's presence depends on, perhaps in a sense derives from, human affirmations. Though strict theological correctness prohibits statements that make God ultimately dependent on human beings, it does not proscribe the idea that God has so disposed matters that human beings may become genuine partners and co-participants in salvation. The concept is indeed fairly commonplace, but the VBMM's statement of it is uncommonly emphatic. Indwelling grace not only transfigures the believer himself, it also gives him the power to participate in the engendering of the same grace in others. The language of VBMM stresses the tangible quality of this engendering. There is no doubt about the concrete reality of what happens.

The remarkable concreteness with which VBMM invests mystical theology clearly owes something to sacramental spirituality. Oblique references to the Eucharist appear frequently enough in the work to warrant attention. For example, the peculiar phrasing of the last sentence in Chapter VI, quoted above, — 'she came to the supper of the Lord' — abruptly changes the point of view. Before that, the text had interpreted the feast on a literal level as the dinner Simon the Pharisee prepared for Jesus. Here, however, the feast is Christ's supper, a eucharistic meal. The next chapter pursues this change of perspective in a passage which associates a feast with images of indwelling grace. Having rebuked Simon for condemning Mary, Jesus turns to the penitent woman:

> Then, turning from the table and facing Mary, in whose heart he found a more joyous feast than that at the table, he saw in her eyes the reflection of his own gracious face, and looked on her with kindness and serenity. (ll. 280-284.)

The true eucharistic feast is in the heart of the believer, in whom the presence of Christ is so real that it can be seen through the 'windows of the soul', the eyes. This image of Christ feasting with Mary Magdalene at the table of contemplation appears a few other times in VBMM. The implication is that the presence of Christ in the believer's heart is as real as his presence in the communion host, and that the transmission of faith from one believer to another is as real as the passing on of Christ in the distribution of the eucharistic elements.

The concept of indwelling grace here appropriates the

ideas of eucharistic theology, but it does not represent a competing theology of grace that denies the efficacy of the sacraments. There is no sign of such a heresy in VBMM. Yet the real emphasis is on the Word, not on the Sacrament, as the vehicle of grace. In the passages discussed above, the actions of speaking and hearing are particularly important. Mary's conversion begins when she *hears* about the prophet. The believer becomes Christ's 'mother' when he *preaches* Christ's word. With this notion, as with the notion of human participation in salvation, VBMM takes a commonplace and gives it an unusual emphasis, spelling out the mystical significance of speaking and hearing at unusual length.

God's prevenient and indwelling grace is the source, and love the power, of a person's growth toward God, but speech — language — is the human means through which grace and love work. And since speaking and hearing have such dignity and importance, an abuse of them for purposes other than their proper ends is particularly serious. From such considerations come the author's uneasiness regarding mere narration unencumbered by interpretation and his declared hostility to trivial stories, exemplified in his comments on the 'tale-spinners' who falsely attribute to the historian Josephus their 'poisonous' fables about the Magdalen's diurnal assumption into heaven (ll. 2299-2321). The author tolerates such things only if they are understood in a strictly 'mystical' sense, a sense in which pleasure in the story itself is secondary to the spiritual interpretation. For these reasons VBMM is, as saints' lives go, an unusually disciplined narrative; on the whole, it shuns the exotic and the marvelous. Descriptions of strange lands, customs, beasts, and people — part of the fun of many hagiographical works — seldom receive much attention. When marvels are told, they are told not to coerce feelings of awe and wonder from the audience but to inform the awe the audience is already assumed to feel. Examples can be drawn from any of the miracles told of Saint Martha.

At first glance, the presence of these miracles in VBMM seems a problem. The center of interest in a *vita* of Mary Magdalene is Mary, not Martha, but none of the many wonderful miracle stories regarding Mary is used, and one of the most famous of them — the one about her being elevated daily into heaven — is censured. Yet, in the chapter immediately following this censure, the delightful story of Martha subduing the dragon Tarascus is told with verve and relish and not much glossing. Another miracle of Martha — the raising of the drowned boy — is glossed, but lightly; the narrative is not gobbled up by interpretation. It might therefore seem that the author is willfully neglecting his own strictures and practice when he discusses Martha rather than Mary. But perhaps the inconsistency is only apparent. For one, the subduing of a dragon by the sign of the cross and the girdle of virginity, and of raising a would-be believer who loses his life out of zeal for hearing the Gospel, may have such obvious spiritual meaning that a gloss would be insulting. For another, the fact that Martha is an exemplar of active works whereas Mary is a model of contemplation is important. It is the business of active persons to reveal in their acts the immanence of transcendence, the presence of Christ in the world. It is the business of contemplatives, on the other hand, to strive to bring themselves into the heavenly presence of God. Public miracles are a mode of revelation particularly suited to the active; the revelations of reflection are particularly suited to the contemplative. It is therefore fitting to tell miracles of active persons in detail, but not decorous to tell them of contemplatives. The Martha miracles are therefore not really a violation of the author's sense of the proper purpose of speaking and story-telling. His practice is consistent with the intentions of charity and praise.

### TRANSLATION

The translation presented here is based on the edition

published in PL 112:1431-1508, itself a reprint of Faillon's edition of 1848, based on the late Oxford, Magdalen College manuscript.²² Faillon provides a modern French translation that is generally accurate despite occasional suppressions and that has proved helpful on occasion when the present translator's insight into pronoun reference and subject-verb relationships has faltered. I observe the following conventions and practices:

(1) I have retained the chapter enumeration of Faillon's edition but deleted the chapter headings.

(2) Passages in square brackets are my interpolations or interpolations adopted from Faillon. I indulge in intervention only when the text seems unintelligible or obtrusively awkward without it.

(3) A few bracketed passages in Latin are provided when the Latin is ambiguous or the translator conscious of presenting an extremely loose translation.

(4) I have translated Latin *castellum* as 'village', 'town', or 'abode', though medieval translators usually render it 'castle'.

(5) Latin *familiaritas* I translate 'intimacy'. Though 'intimacy' perhaps has stronger erotic connotations for modern readers than the latin intends, 'familiarity' is too sterile to convey quite the right nuance.

(6) I use the words 'prophet' rather than 'prophetess', and 'apostle' rather than 'apostoless' even when the Latin uses a feminine form.

(7) Although I draw heavily on the English of the Douay and Revised Standard versions of the Bible, I do not hesitate to alter phrasing when grammar or style demand. At times I adopt the phrasing of the *Jerusalem Bible,* The King James Bible, the *New English Bible,* or the Psalter of the *Book of Common Prayer.*

(8) I have not tried to reproduce the rhythmic and alliterative qualities of much of the Latin, an example of which I cite below:

Inter Arelatem et Avennicum, Viennensis Provinciae civitates, circa Rhodani ripas, inter infructuosa frueta et glareas fluminis, ferarum reptiliumque virulentorum eremus erat. (ll. 2331-2334.)

I have, however, tried to reflect the modulation between highly ornamented styles and plain styles.

D.M.

Warren Wilson College

# NOTES TO INTRODUCTION

1. *De Marie Magdalena, & triduo Christi disceptatio* (Paris, 1517 [o.s.]). Anselm Hufstader, 'Lefèvre d'Étaples and the Magdalene,' *Studies in the Renaissance* 16: 31-60, gives a good summary of the Fabrist controversy and its wider implications from which I draw extensively in these remarks. Also see Hufstader's notes for helpful bibliography.

2. Hufstader, p. 39.

3. See Hufstader, pp. 41-59.

4. *XL Homiliarum in Evangelia*, II.25 (PL 76:1188-1196). [A translation by David Hurst OSB will soon appear in this series—ed.]

5. The legend and doctrine developed together: influence works in both directions. For a more detailed account of the development of the Magdalen legend, see 'Part One' of my edition and study of transmission, *A Critical Edition of the Legend of Mary Magdalene from Caxton's Golden Legend of 1483* (Salzburg: Universität Salzburg, Institut für Anglistik und Amerikanistik, 1985). In that study as in the present introduction, my debt to the various books and articles of Victor Saxer (see bibliography) is pervasive.

6. See Hufstader, pp. 55-59.

7. Printed in *Acta Sanctorum*, July V:218–221; also in PL 133:713–721 with variants in accidentals.

8. Étienne-Michel Faillon, *Monuments inédits sur l'apostolat de sainte Marie-Madeleine en Provence* . . . , 2 vols. (Paris, 1848), calls this the 'Ancienne Vie' of Mary Magdalene and prints it in vol. II, pp. 433–436.

9. J. Misrahi, 'A vita Sanctae Mariae Magdalenae . . . ,' *Speculum* 18 (1943) 335–337 and Sr Benedicta Ward, *Miracles and the Medieval Mind* (Philadelphia: Univ. Penna. Press, 1982) p. 260, n. 65.

10. Edited by Misrahi, *ibid.*, pp. 335–339.

11. Faillon considers the part drawn from *Vita eremitica* an addition and prints it in *Mon. inéd.*, II; 445–451.

12. Printed by Faillon, *Mon. inéd.*, II; 437–445, with the title 'Vie Anonyme Sainte Marie-Madeleine'.

13. See the discussion in Saxer, *Le dossier Vezelien de Marie Madelaine* (Brussels: Societé des Bollandists, 1975) 9–10.

14. Faillon prints *Translationis narratio prior* in two parts, *Mon. inéd.*, II: 573–574 and 741–744. A more reliable edition is in B. de Gaffier, *AB* 69 (1951); 145–147. *Translationis narratio posterior* survives in a short and a long version. Faillon, *Mon. inéd.*, II; 745–752, prints the short version. Saxer, *Le dossier*, pp. 236–241 prints the longer version, the one containing the most important material pertaining to the development of the Magdalen legend.

15. Saxer, 'La "Vie de sainte Marie Madeleine" attribuée au pseudo-Raban Maur, oeuvre claravalienne du XIIe siècle,' *Mélanges Saint Bernard* (Dijon, 1953) 409–410.

16. Saxer, 'La "Vie" ', pp. 408–421.

17. *Ibid.*, pp. 411–415.

18. *Ibid.*, p. 412.

19. *Ibid.*, pp. 419, 420. Translation mine.

20. See Mycoff, *A Critical Edition*, for discussion of the problems of studying the transmission of Magdalen texts.

21. Translation from John Gibbs and James Innes, *Homilies on the Gospel of John*, in *A Select Library of the Nicene and Post-Nicene Fathers*, Vol. 7 (NY, 1888; rpt. Grand Rapids, Michigan: Eerdmans, 1956) p. 437.

22. *Mon. inéd.*, II.

# THE LIFE OF THE BLESSED MARY MAGDALENE AND OF HER SISTER SAINT MARTHA

## PROLOGUE

THE CONTEMPLATIVE LIFE of that sweet lover of Christ, dearly loved by him and worthy to be named with reverence, the blessed Mary Magdalene; the active life of her glorious sister, the servant of Christ, Martha; and the friendship of their venerable brother, Lazarus, and his resurrection through Christ: now taken not from modern tradition newly invented, but from the authentic testimony of the four Gospels, publicly preached from the infancy, so to speak, of our faith and believed and honored as Catholic by the Church throughout the world.

Human mouths need not commend a devotion approved by such divine oracles. He who has ears to hear, let him hear what the Spirit says to the churches by the mouth of the blessed evangelist John concerning the magnitude of the love, the greatness of the intimacy, the abundance of the sweetness which was shared by the glorious Son of the Virgin and his friends, Martha, and Mary, and their brother Lazarus. As it is written: 'I love those who love me'. 'The Lord Jesus,' John says, 'loved Martha, and her sister Mary, and Lazarus.' This is the witness which John gave, which the disciple whom Jesus loved above all others gave. This is the testimony which the apostle who lay against the breast of God at supper gave; which the evangelist to whom Christ from the cross entrusted his Virgin Mother gave.

Truly happy, those blessed saints, to whom the holy evangelist has given such reliable, such shining, such evident witness. Which to show more clearly, I

27

have thought it a worthwhile task to explain in detail
what the various but consonant accounts of the Gospels
say regarding these things; and then to expound
faithfully what happened to the Saviour's friends after
35   his ascension, according to what our fathers have passed
on to us and what is left to us in their writings.

So that we might progress more smoothly, we shall
go back a little in time and try to recount in detail what
the oldest histories tell concerning their origin and
40   birth, their upbringing and education, and their
talents and character, for the praise of our Lord and
Saviour and the honor and glory of his friends.


CHAPTER I


In the territory of Jerusalem, on the Mount of
Olives, fifteen stadia from the holy city, facing east, lies
Bethany, the abode of Mary Magdalene, Lazarus, and
Martha, so often mentioned in the Gospels, most
5    famous for the visits that our Lord and Saviour so often
made there, dedicated to hospitality, celebrated for
feasts, illustrious for miracles, memorable for the tears
he shed there, magnified for his procession from there,
noted for his ascension there, and distinguished by the
10   footprints he left there. In this eastern city, Martha, the
venerable hostess and most devoted servant of the Son
of God, our Lord Jesus, was born. Her noble mother,
Eucharia, came from the royal line of Israel. Her father,
Theophilus, a Syrian, was not merely born noble, but
15   indeed took his nobility from a noteworthy title and a
most important office, for he was among the chief
satraps of the province, which was a great honor among
the children of that age, and was governor and prince of
all Syria and of all the regions bordering on the sea.

20     What is more, he was later moved to become a disciple
of Christ by his teaching, and, renouncing his worldly
power, followed humbly in his footsteps.

    Blessed Martha had a sister of wonderful beauty,
named Mary, and a brother of great natural ability and
25     flourishing youth, named Lazarus. Genius thrived in all
three, together with remarkable talent and a complete
knowledge of Hebrew letters, which they acquired in
their childhood. Integrity crowned the goods of nature
and the gifts of art: in each of them there were found an
30     admirable beauty of body, a most winning grace of
manners, and a most pleasing lucidity of speech. Indeed, they could be seen competing among themselves
in appearance, manners, grace, and honesty.

CHAPTER II

    And since they were, as I have said, nobly born
35     and of noble society, they possessed by hereditary right
a great patrimony and also many lands and slaves and
much money. They owned the greater part of the city of
Jerusalem, and three other estates: Bethany in Judea,
two miles from Jerusalem; Magdalo in Galilee, on the
40     left bank of the Sea of Gennesaret, located in a recess of
a mountain, two miles from Tiberias; and Bethany
beyond the Jordan, also in Galilee, where John baptized. Living together in common, they abounded in
delights, and the younger brother and sister desired to
45     have Martha, as the first-born, administer all their
belongings and all their lands, a trust which she did not
insolently abuse, but, bearing in her woman's breast a
manly spirit, performed it liberally. Since she desired
never to marry, her good name flourished. To her own
50     she was sweet and loving; to the poor, gentle and

friendly; to all, in short, merciful and liberal. And, to
speak briefly, the woman was respected and venerated
by all, for she was nobly born, blessed with many gifts,
celebrated for beauty, glorious in chastity, hospitable,
55    generous, and gracious to all. Such was Martha.

Now Mary, from the time she became a woman,
shone in loveliness and bodily beauty: handsome, well-
proportioned, attractive in face, her hair a marvel,
sweet in mind, decorous and gracious in speech, her
60    complexion a mixture of roses and the whiteness of
lillies. All graces shone in her form and beauty, so
much so that she was said to be a masterwork of God.

CHAPTER III

But because outward beauty is rarely allied to
chastity, and an affluence of possessions may often be
65    an enemy to continence, when she became a young
woman, abounding in delights and rejoicing in a noble
heart, she, as is usual at that age, followed after the
pleasures of the flesh. Vigorous youth, attractive
shape, and many riches enervate good conduct; a
70    beautiful body and a heart inclined to pleasure breathe
forth false sweetness and profane love; nobility of
blood, grace of speech, and many possessions destroy
the heart's prudence; in short, the hotness of youth, the
desires of the flesh, the weakness of the sex all turn one
75    away from bodily chastity.

Alas! Oh sorrow! Tarnished was her gold, the best
of her possessions, by earthly love! Blackened was the
bright color of her good upbringing by the breath of
carnal desires! Drawn by seductive motions, wavering
80    in heart towards all kinds of illicit things, she perverted
whatever God had given her for the growth of honesty

to the service of a lascivious and pandering life. Sweetness of mind she abused to the peril of her soul; beauty of body to the dishonor of her heart; vigor of youth to the destruction of her chastity. Departed from the daughter of Sion is all her beauty; vanished from her is all the munificence of divine craftsmanship, for she sinned so greatly against the God to whom she owed so much.

90 But why linger any longer over this? The soul of youth is a pilgrim: she dwelt in earthly love only for a time. This younger sister misused herself in carnal delights and wandered into a region of unlikeness. Straying far from God, her home country, in a short 95 while she dissipated the goods of nature and of her upbringing. But as soon as she knew herself destitute of all divine virtues, remembering and seizing upon things as precious as they were numerous, and as great as those which she had lost, she hurried to return to grace.

CHAPTER IV

100 Already had the time of grace come, for in this same time a virgin had given birth; already Emmanuel had come down from heaven, that his work might be accomplished on earth. But he was a pilgrim and an exile —his work was alien to his nature, that God himself 105 should be in doubt, that strength itself should be wounded, that life itself should die. This is wisdom. Whoever has knowledge, let him divide his portion into seven or even eight—that wounds should touch man; that miracles should come from God.

110 Already, following in the course of nature, the child Jesus had attained the years of manhood; already, having been baptized by his precursor in ministry, he

had fasted forty days, but was afterwards hungry, for he
took upon himself our infirmities in truth, and not
115   merely in appearance, in figure, or in imagination.
Already he had chosen many disciples from that province; already over thirty years old, he had changed
water into wine. From that time, his fame spread because of the signs he gave and the miracles he per-
120   formed, as befitted the Son of God. He worked diligently the work for which he had come, to heal the infirm
and to strengthen the sinners. 'I have not come,' he
said, 'to call the just, but for sinners. Those who are
well do not need a physician, but rather the sick. The
125   Son of Man has come to seek and to make whole those
who have perished.' His fame spread quickly through
all of Syria, into Galilee, to the sea, and to Tyre and
Sidon.

One day, while proclaiming the Kingdom of God
130   in Galilee, he compared the Jews to children at play,
who shout: 'We have piped for you, and you have not
danced; we have grieved over you, and you have not
wept.' Then he said, explaining this: 'John the Baptist
came, neither eating nor drinking, and they said, "He
135   has a demon"; the Son of Man came, eating and drinking, and they said, "Here is a glutton and a wine drinker,
a friend of publicans and sinners."'

CHAPTER V

In the meantime, the Saviour was invited to dinner
by a certain Pharisee, whom our evangelist calls
140   Simon. He lived in the city of Magdalo, I believe, and was
a good friend and a relative of the blessed Martha. As
Jesus was taking his place at table in Simon's house with
many others who had gathered, the news of his arrival

filled the entire city. They were saying that a kind
145 and holy man had come, pleasant and modest, God-
fearing and merciful; friendly, moreover, to the humble, kind to sinners, gentle to the penitent, a patron of
soberness, a lover of chastity. Some of the people believed he was the Son of God and the Christ.

150 This happy news also came to the ears of Mary, the
young woman of whom we were speaking before, who
took from her own country, Magdalo, which means
'tower', her surname, which means 'of the tower'. Her
beauty wasted, she had, as we said before, lost her own
155 innocence and destroyed the innocence of others. With
her attractiveness, flourishing youth, and abundance of
things, she had waged war on all sides against goodness, until, because of her innumerable sins, she was
said to be possessed of seven demons.

160 Mary, drawing faith from the arrival of the holy
prophet, and confronting herself, standing before
herself, turned her inward eyes towards herself and
remembered all her sins and all the precious things she
had in nature and upbringing from the time of her
165 childhood. Recalling all this in her heart, she found
herself far from God and estranged from herself, and
she began to weep. God, to whom all things are
known, poured out for her the wine of contrition that
she might flee from his bow of vengeance. For it is writ-
170 ten: 'If you do not repent, he shall brandish his sword,
he shall draw his bow, and make ready the instruments
of death.' Then, by a sudden and gracious motion of
the Holy Spirit (which blows when it wills and where it
wills, and blows on whom it wills as much as it wills,
175 and has mercy on whom it wills and hardens the hearts
of whom it wills), the young woman was inspired, saying to herself: 'Know yourself, Mary, and remember

who you were, and what you are now, and what you
may become. Blush to see yourself ignobly degen-
180   erated; repent your having so abused yourself; and lament that you have become a cause of scandal. Groan
for having scorned God for so long, and be ashamed for
having responded so unworthily to God's best gifts.
And so that you do not become slack or
185   careless, dispose yourself better, for life is short, death
sure, and your hour uncertain. Strength is false and
beauty vain: on the day of her death a God-fearing
woman will be praised, and his work in her. Fear, then,
Mary, eternal punishment; look back to the supernal
190   judge; turn back before God's accusation; detest your
past life and hurry to a better one.' Thus, thus, through
wisdom, the hawk soars and spreads out his wings to
the south wind.

CHAPTER VI

Rising quickly, Mary took up a vessel of aromatic
195   herbs made of Indian alabaster, which is a kind of white
marble streaked with various colors, and filled it with a
rare and valuable perfume, of a wonderful odor, so
precious that she thought it worthy enough to take
where she intended to go—to the feet of the prophet
200   who bore the reputation of being the Son of God and
whom she already loved ardently. She had a great
quantity of spices and a variety of perfumes, and balms
also, and sweet-smelling liquors of every kind, for from
her infancy she had used such scents as enhancing per-
205   fumes. She bore the vessel of ointments in her hands,
for it is written, 'come not before the Lord empty-
handed', and she also carried something more
precious—a breast full of faith and the hope of pardon.

All the while, she wept bitterly to herself in the out-
210 pourings of a true heart, which God willingly hears.
'Wretch that I am,' she said, 'I have used myself miserably from the days of my youth! See, Oh Lord, and consider how I am made vile! My God, it is enough for me
to leave my sin! I renounce the seductions of my heart
215 and flesh, and the pomp of the world; I detest my
former errors, and promise to amend at once.'

Groaning within her heart and conscience over
these things, she went to the feast, where it was said the
Son of God was in attendance. Nor did she escape the
220 notice of the one to whom she had come, and from
whom no secrets are hidden; for in truth, he came to her
first, through the sevenfold gifts of the Spirit, bringing to
her the sweetness of his blessing, drawing her
to himself, hastening her on her way. And soon, having
225 by his perpetual interdict driven out and bound up the
seven demons which tormented her, he filled her anew
with the seven gifts of the Spirit. Impregnated with
these, by faith she conceived a good hope within
herself, and gave birth to a fervent charity. Her gift to
230 the Saviour, the alabaster vessel, was an outward sign of
these blessed inner motions and of the burning fire of
her contrition. With a conscience fruitfully laden with
these things and with the fullness of her repentence for
her past life, teeming with a devotion pleasing to God,
235 which stirred within her a certain hope of pardon, she
came to the supper of the Lord.

### CHAPTER VII

Then, entering the dinner chamber, Mary looked
about and from a distance saw there at the table the
Son of the Virgin Mary, whom she at once worshipped,

240    prostrating herself. Rising, she reverently approached
       the couch on which the Saviour was resting and stood
       confidently behind the Messiah, from whose paths she
       lamented having wandered. With the tears of her eyes,
       which had once looked after worldly loves, she washed
245    his feet; with her hair, which had before enhanced the
       beauty of her face, she dried them; with her mouth,
       which she had abused in pride and lasciviousness, she
       kissed them; and with the perfumes she had brought
       she anointed them, as once (it grieved her to remem-
250    ber) she had anointed her own flesh to make it more
       seductive.

           At this, the Pharisee who had invited the Lord to
       dinner was indignant and envious, forgetting his own
       fragility and omitting any natural compassion for
255    Mary's misery. He found fault with her and with the
       one who had come to save sinners for coming to her aid.
       Murmuring to himself, he said: 'Is this man really a
       Jew? If he were a prophet, knowing and keeping
       himself above what has passed, and what is present,
260    and predicting wisely what will be, he would certainly
       see what kind of a person this woman is, whose atten-
       tions he graciously accepts, and would not allow her to
       touch him.'

           Replying to the Pharisee's thoughts, God, who
265    sees all thoughts and judges all intentions, said:
       'Simon, I have something to say to you'. And he, with a
       Pharisee's accustomed arrogance, suppressed what was
       in his heart, and, as though he had murmured
270    nothing, briefly replied: 'Speak, Master'. And the Lord
       said: 'A certain usurer had two debtors, one of whom
       owed five hundred denarii and the other fifty. Since
       neither of them had anything with which to pay him,
       he forgave them both. Which of the two had more

275     cause to love him?' To which Simon, like a fool who
        himself plaits the rope that entangles him, unaware
        that the parable was told against him because he could
        not interpret it clearly, responded: 'I think the one to
        whom he gave more.' To which the Lord said: 'You
280     have judged rightly.' Then, turning from the table and
        facing Mary, in whose heart he found a more joyous
        feast than that at the table, he saw in her eyes the reflec-
        tion of his own gracious face, and looked on her with
        kindness and serenity. But before he addressed her, he
285     defended her against the Pharisee. Still looking at her,
        he asked: 'Do you see this woman?' Then, recalling and
        enumerating one by one her services of washing, dry-
        ing, anointing, and kissing his feet, and showing that
        he accepted all of them with great thanks, he openly
290     reproached his neglect to do the like, matching in-
        stance with instance: 'I entered your house invited by
        you,' he said, 'and you did not offer for my feet either
        the water of your well or of the stream, though it is a
        custom for hosts to perform this ceremony for their
295     guests; she, however, has washed my feet with her
        tears, a ceremony unheard of before, and dried them
        with her hair, more precious than any towel. You did
        not offer a kiss or any other sign of love; she, however,
        has done so not once but many times, for since she
300     came in she has not ceased kissing my feet. You did not
        anoint my head with oil, which would have been a sign
        of devotion; she, however, has anointed my feet not
        merely with oil but with water mixed with balsam per-
        fume. Because of this, I say to you, she is forgiven many
305     sins and is deserving of it, for she has loved much. He,
        however, who has been forgiven little loves little,
        although he should not love God less whom God has
        kept from falling into sin.'

CHAPTER VIII

The Saviour knew that with these words he had
310   filled Mary with great joy and gladness. For her joy was
great when she heard Christ enumerate and praise the
obsequies she had rendered him; and it grew greater
when he said that he valued her devotions more than
Simon's feast; and it reached its height when he pro-
315   claimed that her radiant love was seen by God and that
her sins were forgiven. Allaying her tears and her
ceaseless kissing of his feet with great cheerfulness and
ineffable sweetness, he said to her: 'Your sins are
forgiven. The ardor of your love has burnt away the cor-
320   ruption of your sins.'
Hearing this, the guests who were at table were
scandalized and began to say among themselves: 'Who
is this who even forgives sins? This work belongs to God
alone.' Leaving to themselves those who were ponder-
325   ing these things, the Saviour turned to Mary and said:
'Your faith, which gave you confidence to seek what
you have asked for humbly, has saved you: go in peace.'
Mary, comforted by this favorable sentence, worshipped the Saviour, and, suddenly filled with inef-
330   fable joy, having left the dinner chamber, returned
home, bearing in her heart the seven gifts of the Spirit,
her tears not entirely suppressed, but diminished, for at
first she wept in the bitterness of penance, but afterwards in the joy of forgiveness. The flowing stream
335   made glad the city of God, that is to say, Mary's heart,
in which the Most High sanctified the tabernacle of
God. From that moment, there was no corruption,
either of soul or body, within her; from that moment,
she was the most chaste of women; from that moment,
340   she vanquished nature and triumphed over herself;

from that moment, she so abandoned her former conduct that within her there was nothing but good —
there was no portion of evil. As much as Mary's goodness is known to have been, so much ought we to speak
345 worthily of her. This only do I hold myself worthy to say
in her praise: that I have not the power to praise her
worthily.

CHAPTER IX

After this, our Lord and Saviour made his way
through cities and towns with his twelve apostles,
350 preaching the Kingdom of God. Noble women followed after them, among whom was the first servant
[*premiceria*] and special friend of our Lord and Saviour,
Mary Magdalene, along with Joanna and Susanna and
many others who provided for the Saviour's needs and
355 those of his apostles out of their own means with affection and religious care, accepting in return his blessing,
for he had cured them of evil spirits and infirmities.
Summoned to the bedside of the twelve-year-old
daughter of Jairus, a prince of the Synagogue, he raised
360 her from the dead, saying: 'Little girl, get up.'
Then he commanded them to give her something to
eat. Accepting the faith of the Syrophoenician woman,
he healed her daughter of a demon. He cured a woman
afflicted with a flux of blood by the touch of his gar-
365 ment, and greatly commended her faith.
That woman was from the city of Caesaria Philippi
and was called Martha. Even today her house can be
seen, before whose door stands a pedestal, visible to all,
on which can be seen clearly a bronze image of that
370 woman, humbly kneeling and holding out a palm in
supplication. There stands nearby another statue, cast

in bronze, of a man dressed in an ornate robe draped all around him, reaching out his right hand to the woman. At the feet of this statue there grows out of the base a

375  certain herb, an unusual species, which grows upwards to the hem of the bronze robe. When the top of the growing herb touches the hem, the plant acquires from thenceforward the power of driving out all sicknesses and languors, so that by drinking a little juice of that

380  healing plant, a person can dispel them completely. If the herb is plucked before the stem touches the bronze, it shows none of these powers. It is said that this statue was made to resemble our Lord Jesus Christ, and it is no wonder if, for the benefits she received from the

385  Saviour, the woman wished to build such a monument. It is a custom taken from the gentiles which Christians observe to this day with no difficulties of conscience, to honor in this way those whom they think worthy, to preserve for the memory of posterity old

390  monuments in which are shown their honor and love.

CHAPTER X

About this same time the Saviour was transfigured on Mount Tabor in Galilee. And as the days of his pilgrimage were drawing to a close, he set his face towards Jerusalem and went there, seeking out with an unper-

395  turbed spirit the place where it was decreed he would suffer. Along the way he entered a certain town, that is, the town of Magdalo, the possession of Mary Magdalene and the place after which she was named. There Martha welcomed him and prepared all that belongs to

400  hospitality and feasting, giving to him her heart as well as her goods. There were with our Lord and Saviour the twelve apostles, and the seventy-two disciples, and a

multitude of noble women.

405 While Martha busied herself with domestic cares, her most holy sister chose to sit at the feet of the Saviour and to hear his words, excelling in this greater service her sister, who was distracted with much serving. But Martha came to the Saviour and said: 'Lord, do you not care that my sister has left me to serve alone?

410 Tell her to help me.' Hearing this, Mary said nothing about her sister's complaints, but left her defense to the Saviour, who was now feasting with her at the table of contemplation. For it is written: 'I sit in the shadow of my beloved, and the fruit of his lips is sweet to my taste.

415 Remembering this in my heart, I shall hope in the same.' And the Saviour, replying, said to her: 'Martha, Martha, you are troubled.' The repetition of her name is a sign of love. He loved both sisters with a wonderful affection — Martha, for her alms-giving and religious

420 deeds; Mary, for her unwavering contemplation. 'You are troubled,' he said, 'in tending to domestic things, and you burden yourself with the needs of the sick and afflicted. Before all else, one thing is necessary: to adhere firmly to God. This is the best part; this sister of

425 yours, Mary, has chosen that which shall not be taken from her — the part of contemplation, love, and devotion. And she shall never abandon what she has faithfully begun here, a service which shall have its final consummation in heaven.'

430 He spoke, then took his place at table, together with the twelve apostles, the seventy-two disciples, and the faithful women; and there they were served by the most blessed Martha, generously, as was her custom; and by the excellent Marcella, the chief caretaker of her

435 house; and also by Susanna and by Joanna, whose husband was steward and procurator of the kingdom of Antipas, tetrarch of Galilee.

CHAPTER XI

After this, the Saviour, journeying through the
cities and towns of Galilee, returned often to Magdalo,
440     and together with his blessed company, stayed with
Martha and Mary. The sisters ministered to all his needs
obligingly, with a free spirit, out of their own means.
If, as sometimes happened, household affairs required
that they stay behind at home while the Lord was
445     preaching far off, they sent whatever supplies they
believed the Saviour and his followers needed to have
replenished, which offerings were handed over to
Iscariot, one of the twelve, who, having care of the
purse, carried what was sent, but secretly and furtively
450     took some for himself.

One day, when the Saviour had cured a demoniac
who was both blind and mute, a crowd came running,
marvelling and loudly praising God. The Pharisees
blasphemed and slandered him, saying he had done it
455     through the power of Beelzebub, but the Saviour
answered them by proclaiming that he cast out demons
by the finger of God. To that place came the Queen of
Heaven, with her sisters and relatives, to see and speak
with the Saviour, the Son of God. But since she could
460     not come to him because of the crowd, a certain person
who was by the door got up and said to the Saviour, not
openly nor plainly, but insinuatingly, as though he
preferred flesh and blood to the works of the spirit: 'Behold, your mother and brothers stand at the door ask-
465     ing for you.'

Hearing this, the Saviour did not go out, but
pretended not to know his mother — not that he scorned
his mother, but to reply to the insinuation. 'Who is,' he
said, 'my mother, and who are my brothers?' And ex-
470     tending his hands over his disciples, he said: 'Behold,

my mother and my brothers. Through a special unction, anyone, whether man or woman, who does the
will of my Father who is in heaven is my brother, and
my sister, and my mother. He gives birth to me who,
475     hearing me in his heart, preaches me; he becomes my
mother, whose voice engenders the love of me in
others.' At these words, the multitude of men and
women who believed in him rejoiced.

There was present at that place, along with other
480     religious women who ministered to the Saviour, Marcella, of whom we spoke before, the follower and procuress of the blessed Martha, a woman of great devotion and faith. Believing in the Incarnate Saviour with
wonderful sincerity, trust, and confidence, she con-
485     founded the chief priests and Pharisees by raising her
voice above the crowd and crying aloud to the Saviour:
'Blessed is the womb that bore you, the woman who
gave you out of her flesh the seed that formed the
substance of your body; and blessed are the breasts that
490     gave you suck, the woman whose flesh was the source of
that milk which nourished your flesh!' To which the
Saviour said: 'Not only is that mother blessed, who, as
you say, engendered with her flesh and fed with her
milk the one who is the Word of God; but also blessed
495     are they who, hearing my word, conceive the Word of
God in the womb of their souls. They rejoice in the
same gift of grace if, having received the seed of the
Word by faith, they keep it and nourish it with the
breasts of hope and charity.'

CHAPTER XII

500     On the fourth day of the Feast of Tabernacles,
Jesus went up to the Temple and taught. When evening

came, he went out with his disciples and climbed the
Mount of Olives and came to Bethany, the dwelling of
Mary and Martha, where his friend Lazarus was, and
505   stayed with them, for since the time they became worthy of his friendship, he visited them often, sometimes
in Magdalo, a city of Galilee; sometimes in Bethany,
beyond the Jordan; and sometimes in Judea, in
Bethany, near Jerusalem. Oh truly happy and most
510   blessed, those who were worthy to have such a guest, to
feast on the bread of angels, on the bread by which they
were fed!

On the eighth day of the Feast of Tabernacles, the
Saviour, going down from Bethany, came at daybreak to
515   the Temple, and all the people went to him, and he sat
and taught them. In this place he delivered, with mercy
and wisdom, a sinful woman from the peril of death.
Although it seems a slight digression, we shall nevertheless refer briefly to this event.

520   The Saviour pleased the people greatly by commending mercy and religious charity. The Pharisees,
however, always envied and slandered him because he
received sinners. Hoping to seize on something from
his lips by which he could justly be blamed or con-
525   demned, they led to him a woman they had just taken
in adultery, saying among themselves: 'Let us test him
to see if he will speak against justice on behalf of mercy.
If he says the adultress should be stoned, the people
will condemn his teaching, for he shall have spoken
530   against his own word. If he says she should be freed, let
us cry out: "He is an enemy of the Law of Moses and of
God; he deserves to die." And let us stone him with the
adultress.' Then, coming to him, they said: 'Master,
this woman has been taken in adultery. The Law of
535   Moses commands that such be stoned. What do you
say?'

To this, the Wisdom of God and God himself did
not reply at once nor did he give judgement at once,
but he turned away and sat down. Bending over, he
540   wrote in the dust with his fingers the sins of those who
accused the sinner. It was indeed fitting that he who
had no sin should write them down. In this, the Saviour
gave us a useful example that whenever we hear evil we
should not judge immediately, but should first de-
545   liberate within ourselves by the finger of discretion
whether we might ourselves fall into similar or worse
evils, or whether we are capable of falling into them.

In the meantime, the Pharisees asked him again,
seeking his answer, mocking and jeering, thinking
550   there was no way he could escape, for either he would
judge against justice or against mercy. But in truth,
there is no wisdom, nor prudence, nor counsel against
God. Christ rose to pronouce sentence. Declaring that
those who would condemn the guilty ought to be
555   righteous themselves, he rose, and without offending
against mercy, rendered a just judgement: 'He who
among you is without sin, let him cast the first stone.'
Having thus delivered a wise sentence, he bent over
again and wrote in the dust, again turning his face
560   away, so that the Pharisees might be free to leave; for he
knew that they now wanted to get away to confer once
more among themselves. In this, he instructs us also,
that, having given sentence, we should again bend
down and write; that is to say, we ought to judge our-
565   selves not only before but also after giving judgement,
humbly examining our consciences in fear to see
whether we do not ourselves deserve a like sentence.

Overcome with confusion, the Pharisees departed;
mercy and compassion stayed behind, standing in the
570   midst. Then the Saviour delivered the sentence of

mercy, as before he had delivered that of justice. 'Woman,' he said, 'where are those who accused you? Have I
put them to flight? Has anyone condemned you?' She
said: 'No one, Lord, for none of them was without sin. But
575      you, who alone are without sin, you have the power to
condemn me if that is your will.' To which the Saviour
replied: 'No one, you say? Neither do I condemn you
for what you have been. Go. Look to the future, and sin
no more.'

### CHAPTER XIII

580      It was now the middle of winter, the fifteenth day
of the month of Kislev, and the Feast of Dedication was
being celebrated in Jerusalem. The Saviour walked in
the Temple, in the portico of Solomon, where he
preached and said: 'I and the Father are one', and the
585      Jews brought stones to stone him, but he escaped from
their hands and passed beyond the Jordan to Bethany
in Galilee, the dwelling of Mary and Martha, where
John the Baptist had first baptized him, and stayed
there. In the meantime, his friend Lazarus had fallen ill
590      in Bethany of Judea, also the possession of Mary and
Martha, his sisters. The sisters therefore sent across the
Jordan into Bethany for the Saviour, saying: 'Behold,
your friend is sick.' 'It is enough,' they said, 'to send
word to one friend that another friend is ill: he is our
595      friend, he loves Lazarus. He will not easily desert one he
is so fond of.'

Hearing the news, the Saviour said: 'This sickness
is not unto death, and shall be the occasion for a
miracle to the glory of God, that the Son of God may be
600      glorified through it.'

Now Jesus loved Martha and her sister Mary and

Lazarus. The one was ill, the others were grieved, but all were loved. By whom were they loved? Jesus loved them — Jesus, the Saviour of the sick, the Resurrection
605 of the dead, the Consolation of the sorrowful. Jesus loved Martha and her sister Mary and Lazarus. Oh happy and glorious generation, of whom the Truth Itself has said: 'I love those who love me'. Rarely in Scripture do we find mentioned by name any believer whom the Lord
610 particularly loved.

When the Saviour heard that Lazarus was sick, he delayed going, he delayed helping, so that he could recall him from death. And therefore he remained where he was, in Bethany of Galilee, for two days, until
615 four days had passed. During this time, a cruel fever consumed the body of Lazarus. Doctors could do nothing; medicine accomplished nothing; there was nothing that could cure the sick man, unless the Saviour should come to heal him. The sisters of the
620 young man sat by his bed, promising that Jesus would come, hoping he would bring strength and health. But the strength of the fever at length dried up his lungs; the vital spirit left him; the embrace of death enfolded his body. The holy sisters wept for the young man, tear-
625 ing their garments. It was indeed woeful to see them, filling the air with their funeral laments, their eyes bloodshot and blinded by tears. Nevertheless, they per- formed the burial rites as was fitting: they carried out the body with pomp and ceremony and enclosed
630 Lazarus in a marble tomb, drenching the stone which closed it with their tears. And since he was of noble origin, and was even more noble at his end than at his beginning — being upright in action, discreet in word, generous of hand, and liberal of spirit — there came to
635 Bethany, to console his sisters, many noble people of

Jerusalem, who were present at his funeral.

CHAPTER XIV

Meanwhile, the Saviour, after two days, said to his twelve disciples: 'Let us go again into Judea.' The fearful apostles counseled the Lord—who had come into the world to die—not to deliver himself to death. They wished to avoid death themselves. 'Master,' they said, 'the Jews have just now tried to stone you, and you want to go among them again?' Jesus answered: 'Are there not twelve hours in a day? He who walks in the night stumbles, for the light of the world is not in him. But he who walks in the day does not stumble, for he sees the light of this world. I am the day; I am the Light of the World; and you are the twelve hours. It is mine to lead and yours to follow, as the hours follow the day. Therefore, do not prevent me from suffering; do not give me your advice, but follow me if you do not want to stumble.' Having said this, he added: 'Our friend Lazarus sleeps, but I go to awaken him from sleep.' To this the disciples answered, according to their understanding: 'Lord, if he sleeps, he will get better, for sleep is a sign of recovery for the sick.' Jesus was talking of his death, but they thought he meant ordinary sleep. Then Jesus spoke plainly to them: 'Lazarus is dead, and I rejoice for you, that you believe nothing is hidden from me, for though I am not there, I know that he is dead. But let us go to him.' Then Thomas said to his fellow disciples: 'Let us go and die with him.' Here was a true love, willing either to live or to die with him.

Jesus departed and came to them after Lazarus had already lain in the tomb four days. Since Bethany was close to Jerusalem—about fifteen stadia or two

miles away — many Jews had come to Mary and Martha
to comfort them for their brother. When Martha heard
that Jesus had come, she ran to him. Mary, however, re-
670    mained at home. Martha said to Jesus: 'Lord, if you had
been here my brother would not have died; yet even
now I know that if you ask anything from God, God
will grant it; and I know you have power to raise him if
that is your will, but I leave this to you, Lord, as you will
675    it. I do not ask you to raise him, for I do not have such
presumption, and I do not know whether it would be a
good thing for him to be raised.' Jesus said to her: 'Your
brother shall rise.' Martha answered him: 'I know that
he shall rise in the general resurrection at the last day.'
680    Jesus said: 'I am the Resurrection and the Life, and
since I am the Life, he shall rise through me. Through
me he shall rise now, as I will it. He who believes in me,
who am the Life, even if he should die in body, shall
live, as Abraham, Isaac, and Jacob live, whose God I
685    am, whose Life I am. He who believes in me lives even
in death, and he who does not believe in me is dead
even while he lives. And all who believe in me while
they live in the flesh, though they shall die according to
the flesh, shall not die eternally: they shall live in spirit,
690    until the resurrection of the body.' Having said this, he
added: 'Do you believe this?' Though he knew Martha's
faith, he wished her to confess it, for what is believed in
the heart unto justification must be confessed with the
lips unto salvation. She said: 'You know, Lord, that I
695    have believed that you are the Christ, the Son of the Living God, who has come into the world to save it.'

CHAPTER XV

After these words, Martha went and called her

sister saying in a whisper: 'The Master is here and calls
for you.' In these words it is shown that the Lord called
700      Mary, though John, for the sake of brevity, says
nothing more about when or how she was called.

Mary, hearing that the Lord asked for her, got up
quickly and went to him. Jesus had not yet entered the
town, but was still in the same place where Martha had
705      greeted him. When the Jews who were with her in the
house consoling her saw Mary rise suddenly and go out,
they thought she was hurrying to soothe her grief with
tears. They followed her, saying: 'She goes to the tomb
to weep there.' When Mary came to the place where
710      Jesus was, she saw him and fell at his feet and said to
him: 'Lord, if you had been here, my brother would not
have died, for where you are present, no sickness dares
to show itself. In the face of death, the life of one who
shelters you will be preserved.'

715      Jesus, seeing Mary weep, sighed in his spirit and
was troubled within — Jesus, whom nothing can trouble
save by his own will and according to his own will. Today, a sinner sighs in spirit and is troubled and stricken
with remorse when he considers what good gifts he has
720      received from God and how he has repaid God evil for
good. In truth, it is faith that sighs in a man when he
rebukes himself for sin: it is Christ who sighs in him,
Christ who is troubled, for faith in Christ is the
presence of Christ in the heart.

725      And Jesus said: 'Where have you laid him?' They
answered: 'Lord, go and see.' And Jesus wept. Oh lively
tenderness, testimony of great love, sign of ineffable
friendship! Who can, after that, form a just notion of
the mutual love that burned between the Lord and
730      Saviour and his friend Mary, proof of which we see in
those sweet tears? I believe, with reverence, that that

love is incomprehensible to all humanity and to all angels. 'And Jesus wept!' Oh tears most worthy of reverence, not mere tears, but tears of the Son of God,

735 which flowed from his most holy eyes, which fell from his most beautiful eyes, which dampened his most serene face. 'Seeing Mary weep, he sighed in spirit and was troubled within!' 'And Jesus wept!' 'Jesus loved Martha and her sister Mary and Lazarus!' Therefore, the

740 Jews said: 'See how he loved him.' Some of them, nonetheless, also said: 'Can not this man, who opened the eyes of one born blind, also have prevented Lazarus from dying?'

He could have, but did not want to, for it is a
745 greater thing to revive the dead than to heal the sick.

CHAPTER XVI

Then Jesus, again sighing within himself, went to the tomb. Sigh also within yourself, whoever you may be, who are weighted down with the habit of sin if you wish to be restored to life. The tomb was in a cave, and

750 a stone had been placed before it. Jesus said: 'Move the stone.' Martha said to him: 'Lord, it has been four days and by now the body stinks.' Jesus answered: 'Have I not told you that if only you believe you will see the glory of God? And what is the glory of God? That

755 where sin abounded, grace superabounded, and that whoever has loved greatly will receive even greater forgiveness.' So they took away the stone.

Then Jesus, lifting up his eyes, said: 'Father, I thank you that you have heard me. I have always

760 known that you hear me, but I have said this for the people who are here that they may believe that you have sent me.' Having said this, he cried out in a loud

voice. He cried out in a loud voice because it is difficult for
those who are held down by the weight of their own
765   evil to arise, as the prophet Zechariah says: 'My iniquity
weighs upon me like a talent of lead.' Therefore he cried
out in a loud voice; therefore he sighed; therefore he was
troubled; therefore he wept. And he said: 'Lazarus,
come forth.' And immediately, he who had been dead
770   came out, his hands and feet bound, and his face wrapped in a cloth. Thus, thus is a sinner bound in
interior darkness, in obdurance of spirit — and future
damnation shall deliver him into outward darkness. But
just as Christ himself first delivered him from the
775   inward bonds of death, as it were, so he commanded the
disciples to deliver him from the outward bonds. And
he said to them: 'Free him and let him go. For in truth, I
have said: "You are gods"; and "Do not revile the gods";
and "You shall become the slaves to the gods
780   that you may become free."'
        They are wrong, therefore, who say that only God
can forgive sins and that in this work man may not participate; who, against the command of God, revile the
gods; who try to abrogate the power God has given
785   them. [They cite the Scriptures:] 'Only God is good';
'only God performs miracles'; 'only God forgives sins',
[but these Scriptures mean only that] without God, no
one is good; without God, no one does miracles; without
God, no one can forgive sins. For if no one is good, save
790   God; if no one does miracles, save God; if no one can
forgive sins, save only God, then what is meant when it is
said of the just Joseph: 'He was a good man and just?' Or
what of that blessed man of whom it is written: 'He did
miracles in his own life'? Or what of Christ himself, who
795   said: 'The sins of those whom you forgive are forgiven'?
No. On the contrary, what man does through God, God

truly does, and — what is better and of greater truth —
what God does through man, man truly does. For God
has not said to Peter: 'Whatever is first set free in heaven
800    you shall afterwards set free on earth', but the opposite.
Therefore, the sentence of heaven does not precede the
sentence of Peter, but follows after it. Nonetheless, in
giving to man the power to forgive sins, God has done
nothing more than forgiven them himself through man.
805    And if a man truly repents of his sins, but cannot go to
confession, I say with confidence, that what mortal
priests could not accomplish, the sovereign priest accom-
plishes, and that the Lord considers as done whatever
a man truly wanted but was not able to do, provided that
810    necessity, and not scorn for confession, prevented him.

CHAPTER XVII
Many were the Jews who had come to Mary, and
had seen what Jesus did, and believed him. Some of
them, however, went to the Pharisees and told them
what Jesus had done. Therefore the chief priests and
815    Pharisees assembled in council, and there Caiphas, the
High Priest, prophesied that Jesus would die for the
Jewish people. From that day on, they planned — not
tentatively as before, but in earnest — how they might
put him to death. Jesus therefore no longer walked
820    about openly among the Jews, but went to a place close
to the desert to a city called Ephraim and stayed there
with his disciples.
    Now since the Passover, the feast-day of the Jews,
was near, the chief priests issued a command, that if
825    anyone knew where Jesus was, he should say so, that
they might arrest him. Knowing that they were con-
spiring against him, Jesus, like a lamb going to the
place of sacrifice, returned to Bethany, near Jerusalem,

830 six days before the Passover. He, who created all things in six days, who shaped man on the sixth day, who had come to save mankind in the sixth age of the world would be offered up on the sixth day of the festival, would be crucified at the sixth hour of the day.

835 It was then the solemn day of the Sabbath, and they had prepared a feast for him there, in the house of Simon the Leper, whom he had cleansed of leprosy before this time. Jesus therefore took his place at table, along with the twelve apostles and many others who had gathered. Lazarus was one of those who were din-
840 ing with him, to show that he was really alive and not merely a ghost. And Martha, that most blessed woman, as was her custom, served at the table with a free hand, a cheerful face, and a liberal spirit. Mary Magdalene, of all the servants of Christ the chief, did not forget herself
845 inasmuch as she did not suffer her great zeal and ardent love for Christ to slacken. She took a measure of precious ointment, and, approaching the Saviour with great reverence, anointed his feet as he lay there. That ointment was true and pure, not adulterated with the
850 false ingredients or roots that perfume-makers usually use to defraud their customer's nose and eyes. And it was made of nard, an aromatic plant, which resembles must or cyperum. Its root is heavy and thick and easily plucked though fat; it is bitter to the taste and the leaves
855 are sparse. The tuft of the nard plant ends in a kind of ear, which is used for perfume. Perfume-makers prize both the ear and the leaves. The ointment of Mary, Christ's perfume-maker, was not made of nard root on- ly, but, so it might be more precious, of the ear also,
860 with the leaves added to give strength and pungence to the scent. Nard is indeed the most valued of perfumes, and this ointment was of Indian nard, the most

precious of all, worthy for the feet and head of the
Lord, as three evangelists—Matthew, Mark, and John
865 —testify.

Having sprinkled the feet of the Saviour with the
precious nard, she spread it over them and massaged
them with her hands and fingers; then she wrapped
them gently in her hair, which was of surpassing beau-
870 ty. Drawing them to her breast and lips, she tenderly
washed them. She held them and caressed them for a
long time, then let them go.

CHAPTER XVIII

But this intimacy between our Lord the Saviour
and the first of his servants is small in comparison to
875 what followed.

After she anointed his feet, there arose in her
soul a fire of great love, which he himself had kindled
in her, this woman who ministered to him; who,
trusting in God and in the affection that had grown
880 between them, performed for him the services of friendship, as she had often, if I'm not mistaken, been allowed to do. Worshipping the Saviour, she reverently
approached that most holy head which angels, arch-
angels, principalities, and powers venerate. Drawing
885 back with her fingers the hair of Almighty God, she
broke the alabaster vessel and poured the remains of
the nard over the head of the Son of God. Then,
massaging his hair with her hands, she dampened his
curls with nard. With her delicate fingers, she skillfully
890 spread the consecrated perfume over his forehead and
temples, his neck, and adjacent areas, as though it were
the unction of nobility. In this way, Mary fulfilled the
works of religious devotion that Solomon in his person

895 once sang of in the Song of Love: 'While he was on his couch, my nard gave forth its fragrance.' How sweet-smelling were the hands and lips and hair of Mary from the touch of Christ's feet, whose fragrance surpassed all perfumes! Now was the house filled with the scent of the perfume, as the world would be filled with the 900 fame of this deed. Great was the abundance of the gifts of the Holy Spirit in the spirit of Mary when she enjoyed such intimacy with the Son of God, given to her from above from the Father of Lights.

How pleasing Mary's devotion was to the Son of 905 Almighty God, how sweet her love, how acceptable her worship, the evangelists testify, who say that Judas Iscariot was angry when he sensed what sweetness came from the balm remaining on the feet and head of our Lord and Saviour. Disclosing the ire in his heart with a 910 voice to match it, he exclaimed: 'Why was this wasted? This ointment could have been sold for much, and the money given to the poor.' And he accused Mary, fulfilling in himself what David had said: 'The sinner shall see and be angry; he shall gnash his teeth and consume 915 himself.' He was filled with the demon that walks at midday and the pestilence [*negotio*] that stalks in the darkness, for he disguised his avarice as concern for the poor. He said this not because he was concerned for the needy, but because he was a robber and had charge of 920 the purse — what was sent to the Saviour this thief took for himself.

Now the Lord did not want to endure the grumbling of that traitor any longer, but he did not accuse him of greed. Rather, he heaped praises on his friend, his 925 perfume-maker, and, alluding to his approaching death, said: 'Leave her alone, for she has done this for the day of my burial.' By this, he showed secretly that he foresaw

that Mary would come to anoint his body with perfume, for though she did not fulfill the prophecy in
930    deed, she did fulfill it in desire, and that which one
wills but cannot do God takes as done.

Everyone at the feast cast his eyes and attention on
Mary, marvelling at her friendship and tenderness,
drawing in the fragrance of the nard, and praising her
935    care and devotion. Some of them, however, were persuaded by the words of Judas — not because they were
of the same mind, but because, in the simplicity of
their understanding, they were concerned for the poor.
These people were angry with her and said: 'Why
940    wasn't this ointment sold for three hundred denarii and
given to the needy?' But the Saviour cut them short,
saying: 'Leave her alone. Why do you trouble her? She
has done a good work for me, for the poor you will
always have with you, and when you want, you may do
945    good for them; but you will not always have me. What
she could do, she has done: she has anointed my head
beforehand for sepulture; she has done it for my burial,
preparing in advance my funeral rites. Amen, I say to
you. Wherever this Gospel is preached, throughout the
950    whole world, what she has done for me shall be told in
her memory.'

CHAPTER XIX

In the meantime, a great crowd of Jews learned
that Jesus was in Bethany, and, led by curiosity, not by
love, went there, not for Jesus' sake, but to see Lazarus,
955    whom Jesus had raised. The chief priests plotted to kill
Lazarus (as though it were possible to kill one whom
God had raised after he had been dead four days), for
because of Lazarus many had left the Jews and believed

in Jesus.

960        The next day, the Saviour, mounted on an ass,
rode down from the Mount of Olives amid the ac-
colades of the people, who strewed his path with palm
branches. Seeing the city, he wept over it. Having
entered the city he went to the Temple, cast out the
965        money-changers and merchants, healed the blind and
the lame, and disputed with the priests. But, after so
many tears shed for the destruction of the city (which is
a symbol of the lost soul); after so many loud praises—
'Hosanna to the Son of David'—after the pomp of his
970        procession; after the strewing of garments, flowers, and
branches along his way; after so many miracles; after
the manifestation of divine anger on his face, from
which the money-changers fled in fear; after long
teaching and disputation; he could not, among all the
975        people who had come to the feast, find a place to lay his
head. Such was his poverty that he (who had never flat-
tered or begged anyone for anything) could not, after
searching everywhere, find any inn or any house in the
whole city that would offer him shelter. So, since eve-
980        ning was approaching, he climbed the Mount of Olives
with his twelve apostles to find in Bethany with Lazarus
and his sisters the hospitality he could not find in
Jerusalem.

Going out the next day, he was hungry, for this
985        was his will; and, seeing a fig tree by the road, he went
up to it to see if he might find some fruit on it. Finding
nothing except leaves, he cursed it, saying: 'May fruit
never again be brought forth from you.' He passed the
whole day teaching in the Temple, and when evening
990        came, he returned to Bethany, to Martha and Mary.
Again the next morning, the third day of the feast, he
returned to the city with his apostles, and they saw that

the fig tree he had cursed had withered up. By this example the Saviour taught the apostles about prayer and
995 about obtaining the confidence to ask faithfully for anything, even for the power to move mountains. When evening came again, they left the city and returned to their usual refuge.

On the fourth day of the feast, he went again at
1000 daybreak to the Temple and said much to his apostles concerning the end of the world. Meanwhile, Judas Iscariot had promised the priests to deliver Jesus to them. At length, the Lord Jesus finished his preaching for that day, saying this to his disciples: 'You know that
1005 in two days—that is, today and the next day—the Passover of the figurative lamb will be here, and soon after, the True Lamb, the Son of Man, will be delivered up to be crucified on the third day.' Having said this, he left the Temple, evening drawing near, and re-
1010 turned to Bethany, to his servants and friends, Lazarus, Mary, and Martha. In this he was like the fawn, who wanders far during the day and returns at evening to its old lair. Thus the Saviour, anticipating his passion and ascension, returned to Bethany, which signifies the
1015 house of obedience, thereby showing that he demands of his friends obedience above all other things.

CHAPTER XX

On the first day of the unleavened bread, the fifth day of the feast, Jesus said his last farewell to his dear hosts, Lazarus, Mary, and Martha. When evening
1020 came, he observed the feast in Jerusalem with his twelve disciples. This was that famous Passover meal, that blessed feast, at which he washed the feet of his apostles and changed bread and wine into his body and

blood. There followed soon after the Saviour's betrayal
1025  and passion.

In a garden across the stream of Cedron, one of his
apostles betrayed him with a kiss to the cohort and the
servants of the priests, whom he had brought there
with lanterns and torches and arms. When he was led
1030  away in chains, all of his disciples fled, abandoning
him. But loyalty did not forsake Mary Magdalene. The
skin of her flesh adhered to the bones of the Saviour,
for when Judas betrayed him, Peter denied him, and
the ten apostles fled from him, there still was found in
1035  Mary Magdalene the courage of the Redeemer.

Who can express the sorrow of her heart and the
bitterness of her soul? Her innards turned when she saw
her beloved betrayed by a kiss, bound in chains, and
led away to the palace of the priest Annas, where he was
1040  accused, questioned, judged, denounced as a criminal
worthy of death, spit upon, bludgeoned, blindfolded,
mocked, and blasphemed. Who can recount the tears
of Mary and her laments, when her beloved was led
from the house of the priest to the praetorium of the
1045  governor Pilate, and then from the praetorium of the
governor to the palace of King Herod? Who can tell of
the sobbing of Mary and of her many cries of sorrow
when he was accused by the priests before Herod, questioned by the king, derided by the soldiers, mocked by
1050  the court, and sent back, dressed in a white robe, to the
presence of the governor? Who can speak without tears
of the tears of Mary, which fell more plentifully when
she saw him standing before the judgement seat; silent
before his accusors; repeatedly denounced by the
1055  priests; defended for a long time by the governor, who
worked for his liberation, proving his innocence by all
the evidence, urging that he be released out of respect

for the Paschal feast; the priests, contradicting him, intervening for the brigand Barabbas, shouting out
1060 against Jesus: 'Crucify him, crucify him'?

Then Mary's grief was renewed when she saw the Lord stripped, tied to a column, and flogged with a whip over all his body, to which the column that the Lord was tied to still attests, showing clearly to this day
1065 the blood of the Lord as a certain sign. But Mary's grief and the bitterness of her soul burned still more brightly when Pilate decided to grant the request of the priests, and the soldiers assembled the entire cohort, dressed Christ in purple, crowned him with thorns, placed a
1070 reed for a sceptre in his hand, ironically worshipped him, derisively saluted him, prepared gall and vinegar for him to drink, struck his head with the reed, spat in his face, and at last removed the purple mantle from him, and led him back in, dressed in his own garments.
1075 And bearing his own cross, he went through the city, crowned with thorns. He was followed by the Queen of Heaven and her sisters, and Mary Magdalene, and other women, who had followed him not only out of Galilee, but also from Judea and Jerusalem, and who
1080 wept over him. Jesus turned to these devoted women, and cast his eyes on them, and said: 'Daughters of Jerusalem, do not weep over me, but weep for yourselves and for your children; for if they are doing this when the tree is green, what will they do when it is
1085 dry?'

CHAPTER XXI

Love is as strong as death. This was seen in the Lord's passion, when Mary's love did not die. Christ was led to be crucified and Mary followed, her tears showing her affection. Christ was raised on the cross; Mary

1090    wailed and choked on her tears. Christ was pierced with
nails on the cross; the soul of Mary was pierced with
sharp grief. Christ was mocked by the priests, derided
by the soldiers, reviled by the thieves, blasphemed by
passersby shaking their heads and shouting 'bah!' Dur-
1095    ing this, he prayed to his Father for those who were
crucifying him. In all this, what sorrow was in the soul
of Mary, what sobbing, what sighing, what grief, when
the lover saw her beloved hung amidst thieves. But
nevertheless she bore up under the pain of seeing the
1100    long torments of the crucified Lord she loved so greatly.
Yet what bitterness and anguish she drank in when she
heard the Messiah cry out from the cross: 'I thirst'; when
she saw the sponge soaked in bitter absinthe, myrrh, and
vinegar, placed on a spear-head, drenched in hyssop,
1105    raised to his mouth, and pressed against his lips; and
when, after tasting it, he refused to drink.

   Then Mary's sorrow rose again when she heard the
Son of God say farewell to his mother from the cross,
committing his mother to the care of Saint John, who
1110    was then twenty-three years old. 'Eloi,' he gasped; 'it is
accomplished,' he cried out. 'Into your hands, Father, I
commend my spirit.' Then, with a great cry, he died at
the time he had set for himself.

   After the darkening of the sun, after the three
1115    hours of darkness, after the rending of the temple veil,
after the earthquake, after the shivering of rocks, after
the opening of tombs, after the departure of the cen-
turion and the whole multitude, when she saw the soldiers sent to break the legs of the thieves who still lived,
1120    who can doubt that Mary, her Lord crucified, was
stricken with great fear? Her grief swelled beyond
bounds at that instant when one of the soldiers pierced
the Saviour's side with a lance, and drew it out, and

1125 water and blood flowed from the breast already grown
cold. And, oh, how welcome to Mary was the arrival of
that noble man, Joseph of Arimathea, and of the
prince Nicodemus, with a hundred-weight of myrrh
and aloes prepared for the funeral rites of the Lord!
How gladly she saw the nails drawn from the hands and
1130 feet of the Saviour; his body taken down, embalmed,
and wrapped in linen, his face covered with a cloth.
While all this was being done, Mary stood by, Mary
looked on, Mary wept pitifully and inconsolably.

CHAPTER XXII

There was a garden on the outskirts of the city near
1135 the place where Jesus was crucified. In this garden,
Joseph, a noble decurion, had built a tomb for himself,
round, dug out of a cliff, and red and white in color. It
was high enough that a man standing on the floor inside could stretch out his hand and just touch the ceil-
1140 ing. Facing east were the door and entry chamber; to
the north was the mausoleum itself, raised above the
floor, dug out of the same stone, seven feet long. This
side of the tomb had not been hollowed out but was
solid; the southern side was open. Having wrapped and
1145 embalmed the body of the Saviour, they brought it
through the eastern entrance and carried it to the
southern part. They laid the body on its back, as the
custom was, with the solid northern wall to the left of
his head and the open part to the right. Having done
1150 this with all speed so that the sabbath evening would
not overtake them, they left the tomb with many tears
and great sorrow of heart. And the men who had come
there rolled a great stone in front of the entrance of the
tomb and returned home. But Mary Magdalene and
1155 her companions sat facing the sepulchre, mourning and

lamenting the Lord. Then, noting carefully the location of the tomb and intending to come back to it soon, they went to the city, to the perfume-sellers, to buy precious aromatic herbs and balms, and kept them in their
1160    houses until the second evening of the sabbath. But no matter how inconsolably they mourned, nor however grievously they sighed out their laments, nothing could relieve the greatness of the grief in the memory of this devoted friend.
1165    The Day of Preparation had come, and the sabbath was approaching, so the priests asked Pilate the governor to set guards before the sepulchre: otherwise, a new error might grow up, worse than the one before. He said to them: 'Yours is the error before and after. It's
1170    enough for you that I consented to you in his death. You have your own guards; use them if you want.' The Jews therefore went and secured the tomb, sealing the stone and setting up guards.

CHAPTER XXIII

It was now the great day of the sabbath, and the
1175    tormented body of Christ rested in hope of the resurrection without any blemish of corruption. Mary Magdalene also observed the sabbath, as was her custom, and kept silent, for inward weeping and outward tears do not befit the sabbath. But when the sabbath eve-
1180    ning she was waiting for came, she, along with Joanna and Susanna and the other Marys, her companions, began to crumble the rare and precious perfumes and balms and to mix them with the richest varieties of all the fragrant powders of the perfume-sellers. Thus a
1185    man's soul was manifested in a woman, when she fulfilled in action what King Solomon had sung in his person: 'My hands dripped with myrrh; my fingers were

covered with the choicest myrrh and aloes and with the finest spices.'

1190 While they were mixing, there repeatedly burst from her eyes tears, the perfume of the heart, because of the fond remembrance of her beloved. Her heart enkindled by the fire of love, she relieved the fullness of her devotion by letting it break out from within

1195 through her eyes. Behold, the spices were dampened by the moisture from her eyes; tears, shaken off little by little by her sighing, were mixed with the perfumes; her hands were bathed in the showers from her eyes; droplets flowed from her eyelids — each of them more

1200 dear and more pleasing to God than any fragrant herb.

Most surely, the night of the Lord's resurrection was made famous, bright, and shining by her works of devotion — by the most illustrious perfume-maker of the Saviour and her companions. From then on, God,

1205 the Creator of Time, willed that the order of time be reckoned differently, with night succeeding day.

CHAPTER XXIV

After that sorrowful Sabbath, the happy day dawned. The sun rose from the inferior regions, ascending in a straight course from the East, and brightened

1210 the heavens, preceded by the rose-colored light of dawn, while the true Sun of Righteousness, the Christ, ascended victorious from the nether regions, and, at the hour he had ordained, rose from death to immortality. In that hour, the earth shook with a great

1215 tremor, and many bodies of the saints who were asleep arose. Meanwhile, Mary Magdalene filled an alabaster vessel with noble balms mingled with rare and excellent liquors, completing her preparations before daybreak. So precious were her spices that they were worthy to

1220     anoint the one who is worth more than all the world; so
         plentiful were they that they would suffice to embalm
         his body. And at daybreak, before the darkness had
         lifted, her arms full of perfumes, she ran quickly to the
         sepulchre of the Saviour, though even the greatest
1225     haste seemed slow to her. In the fervor of her love she
         scarcely could endure one night's delay. The other
         Marys — Mary Cleophas and Mary Salome — and Joanna
         and Susanna, and others who were with them, followed
         after the first servant of the Saviour, the Magdalen,
1230     each carrying the perfumes she had prepared. The
         evangelists describe the times of their visitation dif-
         ferently, not from error or negligence, but by design, to
         show the diligence with which they ran to and fro
         repeatedly, coming and going, not suffering them-
1235     selves to be long absent or far away from the sepulchre
         of the Saviour. Therefore, so that I might not wander
         even a little from the sense of the evangelists, I have
         taken care to relate each of their accounts, placing their
         names at the beginning of each passage. This seems a
1240     better course than others have followed, for some com-
         mentators have grouped all the appearances of the
         angels together, thereby conflating what each of the
         evangelists has told differently. They have scarcely
         agreed in concluding that the angels appeared to the
1245     Marys not four times, or three times, but twice, as
         though it were a thing impossible to God and unfitting
         of such a solemn occasion that there be at least six
         angels attending at Christ's resurrection or appearing to
         the women: one sitting at the entrance, according to
1250     Matthew; another sitting within, according to Mark;
         two who were seen by the Magdalen alone, according to
         John; [and two within who were seen by the Magdalen
         and the other women, according to Luke].
         *Matthew:* The Sabbath having passed, on the first day

1255 of the week (the method of reckoning the sequence of days having been changed in honor of the resurrection), Mary Magdalene and the other Marys came to see the sepulchre.

*Mark:* And very early in the morning on the first day of
1260 the week, Mary Magdalene, and Mary Jacobi, and Salome came to the tomb just at the rising of the Sun of Righteousness, the Christ, after the sunset of the flesh. And they said to each other: 'Who will roll the stone away from the entrance of the tomb for us?' For it was
1265 very large. And when they came near the tomb, they saw that the stone had been rolled away and that the Saviour had already broken out of the tomb, closed and sealed with the seals of the priests, just as he had entered into the world through the sealed womb of a
1270 virgin, of which the tomb is a symbol. For this reason it is written that the one who had rolled away the stone was sitting on it. The guards had run away for fear of him and fallen in a dead faint. The angel's face shone brilliantly and his garments glittered like snow.

CHAPTER XXV

1275 *John:* Mary Magdalene came to the tomb early in the morning when it was still dark and saw that the stone had been rolled away. Fearing that his body had been taken away, as the linen left behind seemed to show, she was troubled in spirit and anxious. And she ran
1280 quickly and went to Simon Peter and the other disciple whom Jesus loved, seeking them out and speaking sorrowfully to them. She said: 'They have taken my Lord from the tomb and I do not know where they have laid him.' Here, where it is written: 'They have
1285 taken the Lord from the tomb,' the Greek books read 'my Lord,' showing by this her charity and dutiful

affection. Simon Peter and that other disciple went out
to see for themselves what they had heard. The
disciples ran; Mary followed. The other disciple entered

1290    the tomb and saw the linen grave clothes and the towel
which had wrapped his face folded separately; he saw
the empty tomb and believed that he had been taken
away as Mary had said. Therefore the disciples returned
to their own home, running together. Mary, however,

1295    stayed behind in the place to which she had fixed her
heart so firmly. And she stood before the tomb,
melting into tears, anxious with waiting.

Almost exhausted with longing, troubled in mind
and vision by sorrow and tears, she wept in seeking

1300    Christ and sought him in weeping. She sought him
carefully; she sought him all around; she asked for him,
and not finding him, she punished herself in her eyes
by tears, for her eyes had searched for what her soul
desired, but had not found it. They looked, but did not

1305    see. In a little while, the rest of the holy women arrived,
dismayed in spirit and pouring out their tears. The
angel who had rolled the stone down from the slope
away from the entrance of the tomb and who was sitting on it at the right of the entrance did not make

1310    them wait longer, but, taking pity on their sorrow, consoled them and began to address them familiarly, not
waiting to be asked.
*Matthew:* The angel, replying, said to the women: 'Do
not be afraid; I know that you seek Jesus, who was

1315    crucified. He is not here, he has risen, just as he said. It
is not possible that what he said should not be.' And he
commanded them to go into the tomb, to the place
they had laid the Lord, saying: 'If you do not believe my
words, believe what your own eyes see.'

1320    *Mark:* And entering the tomb, they saw a young man,
dressed in a shining white garment, seated to the right,

in the middle of that place, where they had laid the
the body of Jesus, and they were amazed. He said to
them: 'Do not be afraid; you should not tremble.
1325 Those whom you see are your fellow citizens, you in
flesh, we in heaven [*vos cailibes, nos coelicolae*]. You
are the servants, we the messengers, of one and the
same Lord. Jesus of Nazareth, who is rightly called the
Saviour, who was crucified three days ago, and whom you
1330 seek, has risen. He is not here; he is everywhere at all
times.' The Marys were standing inside the tomb into
which they had entered, on the east side in front of the
grave and the angel stood before them on the right side of
the grave. Stretching out his hand as though to show with
1335 his fingers that the grave was empty, the angel said:
'Behold the place where the prince of the Jews and the
noble decurion placed him, and where the others buried
him with devotion. But since he has risen from death, go
and tell his disciples, who, when he was arrested, were
1340 stricken with fear and forsook him, fleeing, all of them.
And tell Peter, who, when the others fled, followed him
at a distance, and who, after denying him three times and
then being looked on mercifully by the Christ he had
denied, left the hall of the chief priest, weeping bitterly.
1345 Tell them, I say, lest they despair because of their flight or
denial, that he has risen. And [say to them:] "He goes
before you into Galilee, where you shall see him, as he
told you."'
    Then the women left the tomb, running. They were
1350 seized with fear and trembling and said nothing to
anyone. They were greatly afraid.

### CHAPTER XXVI

*John:* But Mary Magdalene stood before the entrance
of the tomb, weeping, more grieved that they had

taken him from the sepulchre than by the pains he
1355 suffered when he hung on the cross. She had lost the
living presence of the one whom she loved so greatly,
and had no remembrance of the dead man except his
remains. Therefore she wept inconsolably, because she
feared she had lost forever what was left to her of the
1360 one whom the soldiers had crucified and whose tomb
the Jews had sealed. Nevertheless — not believing in
what she herself had seen before daylight: the empty
tomb; the apostles with whom she had sought him; the
apostles to whom she had been sent to tell the news;
1365 the women who accompanied her, who had so often
been frustrated in their search for him; the angels from
whom she had heard that he was not there but risen —
she bent down, weeping, and peered into the tomb,
moved and inspired by the very one she sought, who
1370 inflamed her soul with the fire of love and who guided
her in not believing easily in the apostles, or the
women, or even in her own eyes. And she saw two
angels, dressed in white, sitting in the place where they
had laid the body of Jesus, one at the head and the
1375 other at the feet. They said to her: 'Woman, why are
you weeping?' Mary, thinking that they were looking
for him and were not ignorant of the reason for her
tears, replied: 'Because they have taken my Lord' (as
though the fleshly part of him signified the whole) 'and
1380 I do not know where they have laid him. And this adds
to my grief, because I do not know where to look for the
one who can console my sorrow.'

In addressing the angels, Mary had bent down in
the door of the tomb to see better, for the ceiling of the
1385 entrance-way was low, although inside the tomb it was
not. Standing up again, she turned around towards the
east and went out, and she saw the Lord Jesus standing in
the garden and did not know that it was Jesus. Because

1390 she loved him, and longed for him so greatly, and had looked for him so long, and had not found him, her hope of seeing him again had waned by now. This is why, looking all about, she did not know him, and could say with the prophet: 'My eyes are red with my tears, because my comforter is far away from me.'

1395 Jesus said to her: 'Woman, why do you weep? Whom do you seek?' Hearing this, Mary burned with desire, and, heaving a sigh, replied to the one she thought was a gardener. She did not say why she wept or whom she sought (thinking, as many lovers think,

1400 that no one could fail to know those whom they love), but merely questioned him, prepared to throw herself on his shoulders, because she thought he was the one who had carried him away. 'Lord,' she said, 'if you have taken him, tell me where you have put him and I

1405 myself will carry him back.' Oh love stronger than death! Nothing is difficult to those who love truly! The power of the love with which she burned for Christ persuaded Mary that she could carry by herself the body of the Saviour, anointed with a hundred-weight of aloes

1410 and myrrh. To this, the Saviour (who had come to console Mary and who sought her even more fervently than she sought him), seeing her sighs and hearing her laments, which by now had grown so grievous that her vital spirit was diminished from the greatness of her

1415 desire and the multitude of her sorrows, could not bear to hide himself from her any longer. He presented himself, he who hiding himself was seen and showing himself was not seen. And so he called her by name, in the plenitude of his goodness, saying: 'Mary, recognize me, for I

1420 recognize you. I know you by name; I know who you are and what you want. Look at me. Do not cry. I am the one you seek.' In this way he soothed the bitterness

of Mary's sorrow by speaking a friendly consolation with
divine sweetness.

1425 She knew the friendly voice, she sensed the ac-
customed gentleness when he called her 'Mary' in his
usual manner. And at once, bowing her head, humbly
worshipping him, the disciple greeted her master, saying: "Rabboni' (that is, 'Master'). Drawing near to him
1430 to humble herself at his feet — those feet she had embraced nine days before — she heard the Lord say: 'Do
not touch me, for I have not yet ascended to my Father.
Do not touch me with a fleshly embrace, for you still do
not believe that I have escaped the shackles of death,
1435 for though I live you seek me among the dead. First
touch me with the embrace of your heart, believing
firmly in my resurrection. I have not yet ascended to the
Father in your heart, for though I have risen, you do not
believe that I am equal to God the Father.'

1440 Hearing this, Mary doubted no longer, but believed in Christ. From hearing the dear voice of the
Lord and from seeing his beloved face, she drew faith.
The grain of mustard, which Jesus the good gardener
had sown in the garden of her heart, took root there,
1445 growing into a great tree, most steadfast in faith, and
she believed without doubt that she saw Christ, the Son
of God, who was truly God, and whom she had loved
while he lived. She believed that the one she had seen
die had truly risen from the dead, and that he whom
1450 she had placed in the sepulchre was truly equal to God
the Father.

CHAPTER XXVII

At last the Saviour was convinced that the love he
had before taken such pleasure in had never ceased to
burn in the breast of his first servant and special friend,
1455 and he knew (he from whom no secret is hidden) that

he had ascended to the Father in the heart of his
perfume-maker. Just as before he had made her the
evangelist of his resurrection, so now he made her the
apostle of his ascension to the apostles—a worthy re-
1460 compense of grace and glory, the first and greatest
honor, and a reward commensurate with all her services. And he said to her: 'Go to my brothers and say to
them: "The Lord says this: 'I ascend to my Father
through nature and yours through grace; to my God,
1465 under whom as a man I am, and to your God, before
whom I am the mediator for you.'"' He spoke and at
once vanished from her sight.

Mary, seeing herself elevated by the Son of God,
her Lord and her Saviour, to such a high position of
1470 honor and grace; seeing herself alone favored with the
first and the most privileged of his appearances, as being among all women (except for the Virgin Mother of
God) the most tenderly loved, the most cherished,
and the dearest, could not do otherwise than exercise
1475 the apostolate with which she had been honored. She
went immediately to find the apostles and said to
them: 'Welcome me, all you who love the Lord, for the
one for whom I was searching has appeared to me, and
while I wept before the sepulchre I saw my Lord, and he
1480 said to me: "Go to my brothers, and say to them: 'Here
is what the Lord has said: "I ascend to my Father, who
engendered me before all ages, and yours also, because
he has adopted you as his children; to my God, because
I have descended; and to your God, because you have
1485 been raised up."''"'

Behold how the Life, which was lost on earth
through Eve has been restored by him who was brought
forth by the Virgin Mary. Just as Eve in Paradise had
once given her husband a poisoned draught to drink, so
1490 now the Magdalen presented to the apostles the chalice
of eternal life. Eve drank the gall of bitterness for the

first time in a garden of delights; Mary saw victory over
death for the first time in a garden consecrated
to burial. Eve persuaded her own husband with the
1495    promise of the serpent: 'You shall be as gods, knowing
good and evil.' Mary announced to her fellow apostles
the good news of the resurrection of the Messiah: 'I have
seen the Lord,' and prophesied of the ascension: 'And
he said these words to me: "I ascend to my Father and
1500    to your Father."' Mary prophesied with greater truth
than Eve did; she bore far better news than the first
message-bearer did. This change w.is worked by the
hand of the Most High. She came to the sepulchre laden
with perfumes and aromatic herbs to embalm a dead
1505    man; but, finding him alive, she received a very different office from that she had thought to discharge —
messenger of the living Saviour, sent to bear the true
balm of life to the apostles.

Now we shall explain why the Saviour first appeared
1510    to Mary Magdalene alone, according to the testimony
of John and the evangelist Mark. Jesus, having risen the
morning of the first day of the week, appeared first to
Mary Magdalene, and since we read that there were
several Marys, lest we think there were also several
1515    Magdalens as some have wanted to say, he adds as a certain sign of the special honor she received: 'from whom
he had cast out seven demons.' And not only does the
evangelist attest that she was the first who saw him after
the resurrection, but also he says that she was the first to
1520    announce it to those who had been with Jesus and who
were in sorrow and tears. But they, hearing from her
that he was living and that she had seen him, did not
believe it. Unable to persuade them, she ran to the
sepulchre again, hoping to see him again, as indeed she
1525    did.

CHAPTER XXVIII

So far we have spoken of the first appearance of
the Saviour, in which it was his will to show himself to
Mary Magdalene alone before any other mortal, and of
the appearance of the two angels whom Mary alone saw
1530   sitting there and with whom she spoke; and of the
apostolate of Mary, to which she was raised by the Son
of God himself, on a day of such solemnity that none
more happy or more celebrated ever was, or is, or will
be; of her mission to announce the resurrection for the
1535   first time to her fellow apostles and alone to prophesy
the future ascension; and of the draught of life she first
brought to the apostles, which cancelled the potion of
Eve, according to the testimony of the evangelists, John
and Mark. Now we shall briefly explain the appearance
1540   of the two angels, whom she together with the other
women, saw standing at the tomb, according to Luke;
followed by the appearance of the Saviour, whose will it
was to be seen by the two Marys, according to Matthew.
*Luke:* And it happened that while the women, not hav-
1545   ing found the body of the Lord Jesus, stood, troubled
in spirit, two men in shining garments appeared before
them. The women were afraid and lowered their faces
to the ground (from this action originated the custom
in the Church of God of praying throughout the
1550   paschal season with only the head bowed, not
kneeling), and the angels said to them: 'Why do you
seek the living among the dead? The tombs of the dead
are here, but he is not here; he has risen. Do you not
remember how he spoke to you of this?' For he had
1555   foretold that he would be raised not only to men but
also to the holy women. While he was still in Galilee he
had said: 'The Son of Man must be delivered into the
hands of sinners and crucified, and the third day he will

rise.' And the women remembered the words of the
1560    Lord Jesus.

*Matthew:* And Mary Magdalene and the other Marys
left the tomb in fear, and with great rejoicing they ran
to tell his disciples. And, behold, along the way he en-
countered them and said: 'Hail!' By this greeting the
1565    curse of Eve was absolved in the Marys by the mouth of
the Saviour himself, as before it had been in the Virgin
alone by the mouth of Gabriel.

They drew near to him and embraced his feet,
which he had before forbidden one of them to touch,
1570    for she had not yet believed. And they adored him and
kissed the feet of the Saviour. In this they represented
the universal Church. Then Jesus spoke to them, saying: 'Do not be afraid; go, and tell my brothers to go
into Galilee, where they will see me.'

1575    *Luke:* And having gone out of the tomb, they went to
tell this to the eleven and to all the others. Mary
Magdalene, Joanna, and Mary Jacobi, and the others
who were with them reported these things to the
apostles. And it seemed to be a dream to them, and
1580    they believed none of it. But Peter got up, ran to the
tomb, and, bending down, saw nothing but the linen
lying there, and was greatly surprised within himself at
what had happened. Then the Saviour appeared to
him; he appeared the third time to Simon Peter.

1585    *Mark:* After this he showed himself in a different form
to the two with whom he walked along the road and
entered a town, which is now Nicopolis, an important
town in Palestine, sixty stadia (about seven and a half
miles) from Jerusalem. And they went back to tell the
1590    others, who did not believe them.

*Luke:* And they found the eleven together, and those
who were with them, saying to each other: 'The Lord is
truly risen, and he has appeared to Simon Peter,' who

was the first among all men to whom he appeared.
1595 While they were talking about this, Jesus appeared in
the midst of them and said: 'Peace be with you.' And
these are the five appearances of the Lord and Saviour,
by which, on the very day of his resurrection, it was his
will to console and to show himself to those he loved
1600 and to whom he was closest.

And after eight days, he appeared to them for the
sixth time, and commanded the apostle Thomas to
touch his side. He appeared a seventh time to those
who were fishing by the sea of Tiberias. He appeared to
1605 them for the eighth time on the mountain in Galilee,
where, through Mary Magdalene, he had commanded
them to go.

CHAPTER XXIX

So that we do not omit what has excited the admiration of many, and so that we can recall what we
1610 have said at greater length above and our mind can
contemplate it with greater sweetness, we shall consider
how the homage that the beloved Mary showed to our
Lord and Saviour was not kept hidden, as were the
works of other saints (which remain eternally hidden
1615 and known only to the Father of Lights, who sees in
secret and rewards in secret), but were at once pro-
claimed, praised, and magnified by the mouth of the
Saviour; for if by chance some dared to misrepresent or
accuse her, she was excused and praised by him, as the
1620 evangelist Mark says, and received for each act of grace a
hundred-fold of grace in the present life, which afterwards was brought to the fruition of eternal glory.

Her most holy sister had complained of her as she
sat in the shadow of the one she loved, the fruit of
1625 whose lips tasted so sweet to her; attending to his

words, she tasted and saw how sweet the Lord is. Eager-
ly she drank in the waters of life from their very source
in the heart of the one who filled her with spiritual
riches, watering the furrows of her spirit and heart with
1630   the drops of his eloquence, by which holy affection is
made to grow, preparing this holy woman, that God
might multiply the fruit of her devotion. Many young
women have gathered riches, but the Magdalen, the
first of his servants, has surpassed all. The young fawn,
1635   which rests only in a humble and quiet spirit, appeared, reposing in her breast, where it lay down and
rested for a long while, and fed, and found pasture,
and was satisfied with the devotion of her homage.

But without stopping at the joys of the saints
1640   which were tasted in advance by the admirable contemplative, who now enjoys the true joy which had come to
fruition in her home country, we shall recall that while
she was still a sinner she approached the Lord for
the first time in the house of Simon the Pharisee, and
1645   washed his holy feet with her tears, dried them
with her hair, cherished them with her eyes, and
poured perfume over them. The words of Simon did
not discourage her, but, the burden of the debt of sin
taken from her, she was filled with the seven graces of
1650   the Spirit. Happy recompense for homage, never
before heard of!

In a second instance, that holy lover, in the house
of Simon the Leper, broke an alabaster vessel and
poured nard over the feet and head of the Lord. She did
1655   not waste that ointment, as the traitor Judas claimed,
but deserved grace and glory from the mouth of God
Almighty, and received the promise that that deed
would remain in the memory of men wherever the
Gospel would be preached.
1660   Here also, in the third instance, of that celebrated

embalming, she showed not less, but even more devotion, by preparing and carrying to the body of Christ most precious ointments; for although the Saviour anticipated her in his resurrection, he did not spurn her
1665  gift nor consider her worthy of a lesser reward. The divine honors given her were indeed multiplied, for she was glorified by his first appearance; raised up to the honor of an apostle; instituted as the evangelist of the resurrection of Christ; and designated the prophet
1670  of his ascension to his apostles.

### CHAPTER XXX

Mary Magdalene's precious ointments were therefore preserved, divided, and distributed among the disciples of the Saviour as objects of great value. It was not the will of the Son of God that they be used for his
1675  dead body, but rather that they serve his living body, for the Church of God does indeed live, and is nourished with the bread of life. It is the fleshly body of Christ, which does not die. It has been transformed from death into another thing. Mary consecrated her ointments for
1680  the use of this body (that is, for the necessities of the disciples) in offering to the members that which was not needed by the head. The Saviour, source of all holiness, saw not only precious balm in the ointment Mary had prepared for him, but also the great holiness
1685  she had mixed therein; and since he no longer needed anything, being immortal, it was his will that it be kept for his members, whose poverty of holiness might need to be relieved.

Blessed be that soul, oh holy sinner and most ardent
1690  lover of Christ, that, like you, remembers all its years in the bitterness of its spirit and clasps the feet of the judge, and — filled with his mercy, as with marrow and

fat and with the hope of pardon — appeases the severity
of law with the sacrifice of a humble and contrite heart
1695     and a troubled spirit offered up in the fire of sorrow and
true penitence! Such a soul receives from God the gift
of knowledge, as the Lord has said: 'For I have eaten
ashes as bread, taking unto myself the penitent, and
mingled weeping with my drink.'

1700     And even more blessed, oh wondrous contemplative and most devoted servant, is the one who, like you,
moves from clinging to the feet of his humanity to em-
bracing the head of his divinity. [Such a one heeds the
words of the Preacher:] he takes seven parts and even
1705     eight, attributing passions to men but ascribing miracles to God; and he raises up to God for all his blessings
a sacrifice of praise in the voice of exultation and confession; he offers to God, the Father of Lights, from whom
all good gifts come, precious nard of all varieties. He is
1710     anointed with the oil of devotion, and he burns in the
fire of divine love. Such a soul receives from God grace
upon grace, as the Lord has said: 'He shall offer me a
sacrifice of praise. He who honors me, him shall I
honor. But those who dishonor me shall be brought
1715     down.'

But most blessed is that happy man who is merciful and free; who, like you, oh famous balsam-bearer
and first servant of the Saviour, bears in his heart the
perfume of holiness that it may be profitable to the
1720     whole body of Christ; who entrusts himself to the
Almighty; who seeks out diligently the forgotten
miseries of the poor; who pours upon them the balm of
mercy; in whose heart charity burns forever, like the
everlasting altar fire, which the frost of avarice cannot
1725     put out nor the wind of vanity extinguish. Such a man,
through the change God works in him, becomes a god.
Indeed, no change makes him equal with God, but if

he lives in this way, he progresses in goodness towards likeness to God.

1730    It is enough, then, to have reflected on [*philoso-phari*] this concerning the three unctions of the special friend of Christ—the unction of his feet, of his head, and of his body—by which that devoted lover, that admirable contemplative, that happy perfume-

1735    maker gave of her love to the Son of God.

Happy is the one who has heard all this concerning Mary Magdalene with pleasure. More happy the one who has believed it and remembered it with devotion. Yet more happy the one who has marveled at Mary's

1740    holiness, and reverenced her with love, and burned to imitate her. And most happy by far the one who has been so moved by and who has taken such delight in the surpassing fragrance of Mary's deeds that he has followed the example of her conversion, has imprinted

1745    in himself the image of her repentance, and has filled his spirit with her devotion, to the degree that he has made himself a partaker of that best part which she chose.

CHAPTER XXXI

On the fortieth day after his resurrection, the

1750    Saviour, about to ascend into heaven, wished to see and to be seen by his own who were in the world, and so he appeared to them and sat down and ate with them, that through his eating it would be seen that his body was truly risen. Thus, that solemn and happy feast, that

1755    supper remembered through all ages, that famous dinner of angels and men, took place. With the Son of God sat his blessed and glorious Mother, the Queen of Heaven, the Virgin Mary; and the one whom Jesus loved before all others, the apostle and evangelist, the prophet

1760  and virgin, John; and the special friend and first ser-
      vant of the Saviour, Mary Magdalene; and his most de-
      voted hostess, Martha; and Lazarus, whom he had
      recalled from death; and also Mary Cleophas and
      Salome, and Joanna, and Susanna. Peter also came,
1765  who had recently confessed his loyalty to Christ three
      times when he walked on the Sea of Tiberias. And
      among those who ate with him were Andrew, the
      gentlest of all the saints, and James, the brother of
      John, and Phillip, the son of mildness; and Didymus or
1770  Thomas, who examined Christ's wounds closely; and
      Bartholomew, always named in the middle of the
      apostles; and Matthew, also called Levi, the first writer
      of the Gospel; and the cousins of our Lord and Saviour,
      James, son of Alphaeus, later patriarch of Jerusalem,
1775  who was called 'Oblius' and 'the Just', a Nazarene from
      his mother's womb; and Simon the Zealot; and Jude,
      brother of James, also called Thaddeus or Corculus.
      And also many others who had gathered and were
      friends and relatives of Christ in his necessities. And
1780  they were now partakers in faith, of whom it had been
      said before the passion: 'Not even his brothers believed
      in him'. With them the Son of God deigned to eat,
      after upbraiding them for their incredulity: 'I send the
      promise of my Father to you,' he said, 'but stay in the
1785  city until you are clothed in power from on high. In a
      few days, you shall be baptized by the Holy Spirit.'
      Then he charged them with the office of preaching; he
      told them to proclaim the Kingdom first in Jerusalem,
      and Judea, and Samaria, and then, when the Jews had
1790  rejected the word of life, to teach the Gospel through-
      out the world, promising to all who proclaimed him the
      power to do miracles. These things and others like them
      he said to them, like a prince to his people, like a king
      reclining on his couch.

1795     Satisfied with feasting, he rose and went out and led his dinner guests through the gates of Bethany to the Mount of Olives, which is near Jerusalem, about a mile's walk, the distance permitted on the Sabbath. And there, standing before the Queen of Heaven, her

1800 companions the Marys, the apostles, and the whole crowd of disciples, about a hundred and twenty in all, he said his last farewell: 'Behold I am with you,' he said, 'until the end of the world.' And raising his hands, he blessed them. Immediately they saw him raised into

1805 the air and carried into heaven. A shining cloud appeared and hid the Saviour and bore him into the aether, while the lover of God, and the companion Marys, looked on.

### CHAPTER XXXII

    Mounting up on high in this way, Christ led out of

1810 hell into heaven a thousand rejoicing souls of our ancestors; he brought out of captivity all those who had pleased God from the beginning of the world. It was not his will to ascend alone, just as he had not willed to rise alone, but had raised up with him the witnesses of

1815 his resurrection, whose tombs had burst open when the Lord was crucified. Afterwards, when the Lord appeared in Jerusalem, many of them also appeared, and when the Lord ascended into heaven, they also ascended. Indeed, it was necessary for them to rise if they were

1820 to be true witnesses of the resurrection, not fantastical, ghostly, or imaginary ones.

    An army of angels hurried to their triumphant king, and immediately the Lord sent some of them to the Mount of Olives to announce his return to those

1825 who were standing there gazing attentively into heaven with the Queen of Heaven, the apostles, and the holy

women. 'In just this same way,' they said, 'the one you
have seen go into heaven shall come again.'

These things which we have carefully told and in-
1830    serted in the account of Mary Magdalene's deeds should
in no way be considered out of order, for she par-
ticipated in them with all her devotion: just as she
learned of the resurrection in the garden, so she
witnessed the ascension on the mountain; just as she
1835    announced to the apostles the first event as soon as it
had taken place, so she foretold to them the future
ascension; and standing with the apostles at the ascension, as though pointing with her finger to the ascending host, she showed she was equal to John the Baptist
1840    in being more than a prophet. Just as John surpassed all
the saints in his conversion in the desert and his holiness
from the womb, so Mary had no equal in her wonderful
conversion to Christ and her incomparable intimacy
with Christ, celebrated throughout the world. John
1845    called himself unworthy to untie the laces of his san-
dals. This was a great humility. Mary, with her tears,
her hands, her hair, her eyes, and her ointments,
dampened, washed, dried, cherished, and perfumed
his feet. This was a great love. He trembled when he
1850    baptized Christ, not daring to touch the holy head of
God; she poured over that most precious head of God,
worth more than all the world, a precious ointment,
though she herself was even more precious to him. Her
deeds are equal to his, write the four evangelists. He is
1855    praised because he heard the voice of the Father and
saw the Holy Spirit; she, because she loved the Son of
the Virgin greatly, ministered to his needs diligently,
stood nearby when he was crucified, and embalmed his
body, and was the first to see his resurrection from the
1860    dead and to believe it. Christ praised and commended
John's angelic life; he defended Mary against the mur-

muring Pharisee; he excused her to the complaining Martha; he praised her before the angry Judas, and destined her to be apostle to his apostles. Among the
1865 sons of women, only the King of Heaven is equal to and greater than the Baptist; among the daughters of men, only the Queen of Heaven is equal to and greater than Mary Magdalene.

CHAPTER XXXIII

Truly, amid such great glorifications of Christ,
1870 Mary Magdalene outwardly rejoiced with an ineffable joy in the glory of her Lord and Redeemer, but inwardly she grieved with the grief of a forsaken lover for his corporal absence. It is natural, I say, very natural, and even necessary, that fast friends be happy and joyful when
1875 together and tearful and sad when apart. The greatness of love for the one departed is measured by the tears of the one remaining behind; the love felt in the presence of the beloved equals the sorrow felt at parting.

Left alone, therefore, Mary endured what all
1880 lovers endure when they lose each other, though she had not really lost her lover, since he had only gone before to prepare a place for her. In short, who would dare guess what sweetness and what love she felt listening to the Saviour while she ate with him, enjoyed his
1885 presence, and talked with him; or what incomparable light she saw in the Son of the Virgin, on whose face she could not be satiated, who is the most lovely of the sons of men? [And who can guess what sorrow she felt] after the last farewell; after the solemn words of benediction,
1890 when, suddenly raising his hands, he was borne into the air; after the milky cloud reaching up high into the aether took him as she followed him, who would not be brought back to her, with the sharp gaze of her eyes;

1895 and after he was received into the open heavens, within which she could no longer see him? I can scarcely believe, I find it very difficult indeed to believe, that she stood there very long. More likely, she grew weak, fell in a faint, grown pale, her limbs frozen. And when warmth returned again to her breast, her tears reap-

1900 peared and flowed plentifully. I ask you, is it possible that Mary could remember the Lord Jesus, whom she loved so much and who loved her so much, without grief, without tears? Is it possible that from that time on there was any period that was without sorrow, any

1905 moment without sadness, any hour without sighs, any time whatsoever in which she did not know grief, especially when she remembered his promises: 'I go to prepare your place and I shall return' to take them with him so that they could be with him and he with them?

1910 When she turned these things over in her heart, her sorrow turned to joy. When, through constant contemplation, she discerned the presence of the Son of God in spirit, her desire for his corporal presence was .empered and she rested quietly in the sweet memory

1915 of him. And finally, after many sighs, after long waiting, after hungering for that most happy vision for a long time, she was satisfied with the sight of that beloved face. In the rest of eternal contemplation, he gave her his sweet embraces.

CHAPTER XXXIV

1920 Then, after the vision of the angels and their words, the apostles adored the Lord and Saviour in the place where he had left his footprints. Then they accompanied the Queen of Heaven in her return to Jerusalem with great joy, and they entered the temple,

1925 praising and blessing the Lord. And they went up into

the cenacle with the Mother of God, her companions
the Marys, and other holy women, and those who knew
Christ, in great joy, giving themselves to prayer
together. There were about a hundred and twenty of
1930　them.

After they had elected Saint Matthias to the
number of the apostles, the day of Pentecost came and
the Holy Spirit descended upon them at the third hour
of the day in a corporal form, in tongues of fire with a
1935　great noise, and they began to speak in the tongues of
all peoples and to prophecy. And whatever language
they spoke, it seemed to the hundred men and women
who heard them that, whatever their own language
was, they were hearing it spoken. There were then in
1940　Jerusalem attending the feast religious men from all na-
tions and languages under heaven. Among them, five
thousand immediately believed, and afterwards an innumerable multitude. All who believed were equal
and shared all in common. As many of them as were
1945　owners of farms or houses sold them and brought the
price of them to the feet of the apostles and laid it
there. Lazarus, the friend of our Lord and Saviour, and
his sisters Mary and Martha, who possessed a great
patrimony and a wealth of riches, as much in Jerusalem
1950　and Bethany of Judea as in Magdalo and Bethany of
Galilee, sold all and placed the price before the feet of
the prince of the apostles.

The noble matrons and widows ministered with
wonderful devotion and fitting affection to the glorious
1955　Virgin, Mary, the Mother of God, and, in keeping with
the custom of the land, showed due reverence for the
holy apostles of Christ, and were themselves honored.
They were the ones who before had been devoted
friends of the Saviour: Mary Magdalene, the special
1960　friend of the Son of God and his first servant, the apostle

to the apostles; and the most blessed Martha, the daughter of liberality; and the Lord's aunt, Mary Cleophas; and Salome, and Joanna and Susanna, his servants, and the acquaintances of the Queen of Heaven, whom the evangelists call her sisters.

Because of their burning zeal, a rumor concerning them sprang up among the Jews who had come from Greece, that in the daily ministry of the saints their widows were placed behind the women of Galilee and Judea. Learning of this, the prince of the apostles summoned a council; it elected seven deacons and entrusted to them the tables and those who served at the tables. They were Stephen and Philip, Parmenas and Timon, Prochorus and Nicanor, and Nicolas. The blessed Stephen shone in miracles and soon was crowned a martyr. But all the disciples of the Saviour, along with Philip, were cast out of Jerusalem, except for the apostles, who were with the Queen of Heaven, and the illustrious women who served them. Mary Magdalene adhered with unspeakable devotion to the glorious Virgin Mary as Queen of Heaven and Mother of the Eternal King. She served as her maid with wonderful affection, giving herself over to supernal contemplation with her, and frequently sharing in the angelic visions and visitations she enjoyed as mistress, for, as the handmaiden and special friend of her mistress' Son, our Lord and our God, Jesus Christ, she deserved to be rewarded with revelations in visions and conversations, receiving solace for her grief in the memory of the abundant sweetness of Christ. The lover ceaselessly thought of her beloved, and in her meditation she burned with the fire of love, the inextinguishable fire in which she was daily consumed in the holocaust of insatiable desire for her Redeemer.

CHAPTER XXXV

1995     Because of the magnificent, inestimable, and all-embracing friendship she had with the Saviour, this holy woman received the same love and honor that the glorious Mother of God and the holy apostles received. They loved her all the more fervently knowing that the

2000     Son of God, her master and God, had loved her greatly; they honored her all the more highly, proclaiming abroad that the Creator and Redeemer of the world had honored her; they consoled her all the more tenderly seeing that the God of all consolation and solace had

2005     lovingly consoled her, either in person or through his angels. They constantly recalled to mind and frequently preached to the people how she had turned away from worldly vanity to follow the Saviour, and they presented her penitence to sinners—for whom it was

2010     Christ's will to die—as an example of conversion, that they might return to their senses. And because penitence is fruitless and illusory if hope of forgiveness be lacking, they used Mary's faith and trust as a pledge of the certain hope of remission, that they might revive

2015     the penitent. And since to flee evil without disposing oneself to do good does not satisfy God, they held up Mary's life as a mirror of all sanctity, to give knowledge and be a model of good conversion, that the faithful might follow in the odor of her perfume and be changed.

2020     And because the fruit of piety is supernal propitiation and abundant reward, they presented Mary as proof of divine mercy, that from her all might take occasion to rejoice. The apostles also frequently remembered the incomparable devotion of her most holy sister Martha

2025     in rendering holy services to the Saviour and providing for his necessities with a liberal spirit and a benevolence full of grace. They preached to the people how before

all other women these two devoted sisters were
welcome, pleasing, and acceptable to the Son of God;
2030    how intimately they loved him and how sweetly they
were loved by him; how graciously he frequented their
hospitality; how affectionately they ministered to all his
needs out of their own means; how confidently
they called him to their brother — 'Behold, he whom
2035    you love is ill' — how lovingly he revealed to his
apostles the death of this brother, saying, 'Lazarus our
friend sleeps'; and how pitifully he sighed seeing them
sigh and wept seeing them weep, as the Jews said,
'See how much he loved him,' confirming in this the
2040    words of the disciple whom Jesus loved above all others:
'The Lord Jesus loved Martha and her sister Mary and
Lazarus.' The apostles even decided to establish the
house of Christ's friends — that is, of Lazarus, Mary, and
Martha — as a house of prayer, for they recalled how
2045    often Almighty God, the Son of the Virgin Mother,
had walked there, sat there, lain down there, slept
there, passed the night there, prayed there, and performed miracles there. They remembered how the
Saviour had sanctified and dedicated this holy habita-
2050    tion, house, and resting-place [*perendinatione*]. In
that very same basilica they ordained Saint Lazarus as
bishop of his own city for the increase of the number of
the faithful. He, after the savage persecution in Judea,
went to Cyprus and preached the word of Christ there,
2055    and there he sat as patriarch, and lived twenty-four
years after his resurrection. Even today his memory and
that of his sisters is reverently celebrated in Bethany on
the sixteenth kalends of January.

### CHAPTER XXXVI

After the martyrdom of the blessed Stephen, proto-
2060    martyr, Saul was called by heaven to the faith (it was

not until after twelve years that he was named Paul).
And those who were cast out with Philip and the other
companions of Saint Stephen wandered about preaching the Kingdom of God until they came to Antioch
2065    where there had gathered a great Church of disciples.
Here the name 'Christian' originated; here the blessed Peter set up his patriarchal throne, to which
Evodius was raised as patriarch after Peter returned to
Jerusalem with his fellow apostles, where, following the
2070    Saviour's command, they preached in the promised
land for twelve years in succession to the twelve tribes
only.

And in the thirteenth year after the ascension,
James, the brother of John, was slain by the sword and
2075    Peter thrown into prison, and Saul, under the name
Paul, sent by the Holy Spirit as apostle of the gentiles.
In the fourteenth year the division of the apostles was
made. The East fell to Thomas and Bartholomew; the
South, to Simon [the Zealot] and Matthew; the North,
2080    to Phillip and Thaddeus; the middle of the world, to
Matthias and James; the provinces of the Mediterran-
ean Sea, to John and Andrew; the kingdoms of the
West, to Peter and Paul. At that time, Paul came to
Jerusalem to see Peter; and John, James, and Peter
2085    received him and his fellow apostle Barnabas and gave
them the right hand of fellowship, that they might pro-
ceed to preach in Syria and Illyricum. Peter was to leave
the East and go to Rome. He delegated the western
regions where he himself could not go to preachers of
2090    the Gospel, noblemen in Christ and the oldest of
Christ's disciples. To the land of the Gauls, which has
seventeen provinces, he sent the same number of
bishops; and to the land of the Iberians, which has
seven provinces, the same number of doctors.
2095    Of these twenty-four elders, the first and foremost
was the excellent Maximinus, who was numbered

among the seventy-two disciples of the Lord and
Saviour, a distinguished doctor, blessed with miracles
and all graces and after the apostles the standard-bearer
2100    of the army of Christ. Mary Magdalene joined herself
by the bonds of charity to his piety and sanctity, so that
wheresoever God called him, he was never separated
from his comrades and companions.

At this time, the Queen of Heaven, leaving her
2105    work of contemplation, was assumed into heaven to
partake of the joys of Paradise, and at this time were
separated ten of the apostles, who had rested for a long
time in pious devotion, until, the envy of the Jews culminating in a persecution of the Church, Herod struck
2110    off the head of the apostle James, threw Peter into
prison, and drove the believers beyond his borders.
Thus, in this savage storm of persecution, the faithful
were dispersed to seek out the diverse places of the
world that God assigned to them to preach ceaselessly
2115    the word of salvation to the gentiles ignorant of Christ.
Those who departed were accompanied by the noble
women and widows who had served them in Jerusalem
and in the East, and who could not bear to be long
separated from the fellowship of the special friend of
2120    the Lord and Saviour and his first servant in all offices.
Among them were the venerable hostess of the Son of
God, the blessed Martha; her most reverend brother
Lazarus, then bishop of Cyprus; and her sister, following in her footsteps, together with the blessed Marcella,
2125    a woman of great devotion and faith, the handmaiden
of Martha, who in greeting the Lord had said: 'Blessed
be the womb that bore you.' And there came also Saint
Parmenas, a deacon full of faith and the grace of God,
into whose care and keeping the blessed Martha had
2130    commended herself in Christ just as Saint Mary had entrusted herself to the bishop, Saint Maximinus.

Wonderful indeed is the counsel of divine providence which led them in this journey to the western regions of the world, for by it the praise and memory of
2135 the blessed Mary and her sister became known to the whole world, and not by the Gospel alone. For in truth, just as the East is blessed by the example of their devout conversation, so is the West favored by their corporal presence and most holy relics.

CHAPTER XXXVII

2140 Entrusting himself to the waves of the sea, Saint Maximinus the archbishop, along with the glorious friend of God, Mary Magdalene, her sister the blessed Martha, and the blessed archdeacon Parmenas, and the bishops Trophimus and Eutropius, together with the
2145 rest of the leaders of the army of Christ, left Asia behind, sped along by the East wind, and sailed between Europe and Africa by way of the Tyrrhenian Sea, and descended by circular routes to the city of Rome and all of Italy, which they left behind on their right
2150 together with the Alps, which, rising up from the Ligurian Gulf and the Gaulish Sea, stretch eastward, ending at the Adriatic Sea. Turning their course right, they landed at Vienne, a province of Gaul, before the city of Marseilles, where the Rhône flows into the
2155 Gaulish Sea. There, invoking God, the great monarch of the world, they divided among themselves the provinces of the region to which the Holy Spirit had guided them, inspired in this by that same Spirit. And soon they went out and preached everywhere, and the Lord worked
2160 with them, confirming their words with the signs that followed after. The king of powers, beloved of the beloved, gave the word to those who preached with great power; to the beauty of the house of God he gave spoils

of powerful weapons to divide.

2165     To Saint Maximus the archbishop fell by lot Aix, metropolis of the second province of Narbonne, in which the blessed Mary Magdalene finished the course of her pilgrimage. Paul had Narbonne, metropolis of the first province of Narbonne; Austregisilus, Bourges,

2170 metropolis of the first province of Aquitaine; Irenaeus, Lyons, metropolis of the first province of Lyons; [Gatianus, Tours, metropolis of the third province of Lyons]; Sabinus and Potentianus, Sens, metropolis of the fourth province of Lyons; Valerius, Trier, metropolis of the pro-

2175 vince of Belgium; Feroncius, Besançon, metropolis of the province of Maxima Sequanorum; Eutropius, Saintes, a city of the second province of Aquitaine, of which Bordeaux is now metropolis; Trophimus, Arles, then metropolis of Vienne. These ten provinces received

2180 the faith from their preaching. The other doctors preached not only in the seven remaining provinces, but also in seven provincial cities; Eutropius at Orange, city of the second province of Vienne; Fronto at Périgueux, city of the second province of Aquitaine, George at Vetula, city

2185 of the first province of Aquitaine; Julianus at Mans, city of the third Lyonnaise; Martial at Limoges, city of the first Aquitaine; Saturninus at the city of Toulouse, in the first Narbonnaise, where he was thrown from the capitol for the faith of Christ. Parmenas retired to the

2190 city of Avignon, in Vienne, along with the venerable servant of the Lord and Saviour, Martha, and her servant Marcella, and Epaphras and Sosthenes, Germanus and Euchodia, and Syntex. Rouen with its province, the second Lyonnaise, which is now Normandy; Mainz

2195 with its province, the first German; Cologne with its province, the second German; Octodure with the province of the Greek Alps and the Apennines; the metropolis of Auch with its province, Novempopulania; the

metropolis of Embrun with its province of the Maritime
2200 Alps; and the metropolis of Rheims with its province, the
second Belgian, were all reserved for these doctors. And
here are the names of those who were sent by the apostles
into Spain; Torquatus, Thesiphon, Secundus, In-
dalecius, Caecilius, Esicius, and Euphrasius. These seven
2205 brought the seven provinces of Spain to the christian
faith.

CHAPTER XXXVIII

The blessed Maximinus, having entered the metropolis of Aix, sowed the seeds of heavenly doctrine in
the hearts of the gentiles, preaching, praying, and
2210 fasting day and night that he might lead the unbelieving people of the region to the knowledge and worship of
Almighty God. Because of his preaching of the Gospel,
the harvest of the new faith soon sprang up, and the
blessed bishop Maximinus, presiding over the Church
2215 of Aix, shone in the power of many diverse miracles.
With him in the same church the glorious friend of the
Lord and Saviour devoted herself to contemplation, for
she was in fact the most ardent lover of the Redeemer,
the woman who had wisely chosen the best part which
2220 —witness God—was never taken from her once she
received it from Christ at his feet.
Mary hungered in spirit for the Word of God,
which, in a wonderful manner, excited her desire again
and again. Drawn by the sweetness of her beloved, she
2225 became drunk on the cup of heavenly desire, compos-
ing herself and raising herself up so that, dissolved at
last in the heat of a most chaste love, she drank in interior joy. She who before had remained on earth now
walked in spirit among the angels in the spaciousness of
2230 the heavenly choirs. Such were the things with which

she occupied herself. But she was also mindful of the wellbeing of her friends who had come to the western ends of the earth, so from time to time she left the joys of contemplation and preached to the unbelievers or
2235    confirmed the believers in the faith, pouring into their souls the sweetness of her spirit and the honey of her words. For her lips spoke from the fullness of her heart, and because of this all her preaching was a true exercise of divine contemplation. She often presented herself to
2240    sinners as an example of conversion, to penitents as a pledge of the certain hope of remission, to the faithful as a model of mercy, and to all the christian people as a proof of divine compassion. She showed to them those eyes which in weeping had dampened the feet of Christ
2245    and which saw for the first time the Christ who had risen from the dead; she showed also the hair with which a first time she dried the drops of her tears from his feet and a second time, at the feast, she wiped off the precious nard she had poured over those feet; also
2250    the mouth together with the lips, by which his feet were kissed thousands and thousands of times, not only while he lived, but also when he was dead and when he had risen from death; and the hands and fingers which touched the feet of Almighty God, and washed them,
2255    and anointed them, and anointed them again with perfume of nard, and which poured the remainder of the nard over the head of the Son of God.

Have I been the only one to recount all this? What evangelist has passed in silence over the merits of
2260    Mary Magdalene? Who among the apostles clung so firmly to the Lord? Which of them drank so avidly his sweet doctrine? It was fitting, then, that just as she had been chosen to be the apostle of Christ's resurrection and the prophet of his ascension, so also she became an
2265    evangelist for believers throughout the world. This is

what he intended who, when she anointed his head,
saw her devotion and praised it, saying: 'She has done a
good deed for me. Amen, I say to you, wheresoever this
Gospel will be preached, throughout the whole world,
2270 what she has done will be told in her memory.'

CHAPTER XXXIX

The blessed Martha and her companions also
preached to the people concerning the Lord and
Saviour in the city of Avignon and in Arles, and in the
households and villages around the Rhône, and in the
2275 province of Vienne. She publicly declared what she had
seen concerning him and what she had been given
directly from his lips, and she preached about divine
power, and performed miracles herself. The gift of
healing came to her, so that when occasion demanded,
2280 by prayer and by the sign of the cross, she healed lepers,
cured paralytics, revived the dead, and bestowed her
aid on the blind, the mute, the deaf, the lame, the in-
valid, and the sick. Thus did Martha do.
        In a like manner, Mary performed miracles with in-
2285 expressible ease to establish the truth of her words and to
provoke faith in her listeners. Both sisters were reverenced for beauty in face, honesty in conduct, and ready
grace and persuasiveness in words. Never, or rarely, was
anyone found who departed from their preaching
2290 unbelieving or without weeping. None departed from
their presence who was not enflamed by the love of the
Lord and Saviour or moved to tears by the prospect of
his own misery.
        They were frugal in their diet and modest in their
2295 dress. Mary indeed cared little for food and clothing
after she lost the corporal presence of the Lord and
Saviour, but the women who remained attached to her

with a wonderful affection provided enough for her needs. Because of this, an apocryphal story has sprung
2300 up, though it may not be entirely apocryphal, for it is the habit of poisoners to mix in much honey so that they may more easily pass on the gall. Because of this, I say, the false legend has taken root that she was carried up into the aether every day by angels and carried back
2305 down by angels, and that she ate the food of highest heaven which the angels brought her.

If this is understood in a mystical sense, it is not completely unbelievable, for it is a fact that admits no doubt that she was quite often refreshed by the sight of
2310 angels, aided by their services, and delighted by their conversation. And it is fitting, it is very fitting, that the God of all consolation should comfort Mary in a wonderful manner unheard of before, for this same Mary had rendered him on earth services of devotion unheard of before.
2315 But the rest of the tale—that after the ascension of the Saviour she immediately fled to the Arabian desert; that she remained there without any clothing in a cave; and that she saw no man afterwards until she was visited by I know not what priest, from whom she begged a garment,
2320 and other such stuff—is false and a fabrication of storytellers drawn out of the accounts of the Penitent of Egypt. And these tale-spinners convict themselves of falsehood from the very beginning of their story, for they ascribe their account to Josephus, that most learned historian, though
2325 Josephus never mentions anything about Mary Magdalene in his books. Of this we have said enough.

Now let us return to the course of our narration, and leave behind for the time being the contemplation of Mary, and pursue the deeds and miracles of her
2330 sister, the most blessed Martha.

CHAPTER XL

2335

2340

2345

2350

2355

2360

Between Arles and Avignon, cities of the province of Vienne, on the banks of the Rhône, between infertile groves and the gravel of the river-bank, there was a wilderness of fierce and venomous reptiles. In this place, among other poisonous animals, there roamed a terrible dragon of unbelievable length and great bulk. It breathed out poisonous fumes, shot sulfurous flames from its eyes, and emitted fierce hissings with its mouth and horrible noises with its curved teeth. With its talons and teeth it tore to pieces anyone who crossed its path; with its poisonous breath it killed anyone who came too near. It is incredible how many sheep and shepherds it devoured and what a great multitude of men it killed with its evil odor.

One day, as the holy woman [Martha] preached the word of God to a crowd that had gathered, breaking off the talk, which was, as usual, about the dragon, some of the people out of devout humility and some out of a desire to test her said: 'If the power which this blessed woman shows is of Christ, is it not possible that she could do what no human efforts can do and remove this dragon from our midst?' To this, she answered: '[I can,] if you are ready to believe, for all things are possible to those who believe.'

At once the people pledged their faith and followed her gratefully as she proceeded with confidence to the dragon's lair. With the sign of the cross she subdued the dragon's wildness, and with her own girdle she bound its neck, as the people looked on intently from afar. 'What is it,' she asked, 'that you fear? Here I am holding this serpent and you still keep back. Approach bravely in the name of our Lord and Saviour and tear this venomous beast to pieces.'

2365 She spoke, and by virtue of her great power, she
forbade the dragon to hurt anyone with its breath or its
teeth. After that, she rebuked the crowd for its scant
faith and urged the people to kill the beast confidently.
With the dragon restrained in this way, the courage of
the crowd was renewed, and with arms and manly
2370 courage, they attacked fiercely and tore it to bits, ad-
miring all the while the faith and constancy of the
blessed Martha, who had rendered helpless such an im-
mense animal, binding it so easily and without any fear
with her fragile girdle. That wilderness was before called
2375 'Blackhearth' [*niger focus*], but from then on it was called
'Tarascon' for the dragon, whose name was Tarascus.

And so, by seeing or by hearing of this miracle,
the people of the province of Vienne believed in the
Lord and Saviour and were baptized, glorifying God for
2380 the miracles of his handmaiden. And for ever after, the
whole province loved her and honored her for her surpassing merit.

CHAPTER XLI

All of the poisonous reptiles having been chased out
of the wilderness of Tarascon by the power of God, the
2385 most holy Martha chose to make her home there,
transforming a place that had before been hateful and
detestable into a pleasant and agreeable habitation. And
she built a house of prayer for herself, which she proceeded to decorate with virtues and miracles, greater things by
2390 far than all the useless ornaments women admire. For
seven years she stayed there alone, and during all that
time her only foods were roots, bitter herbs, apples,
and the fruits of other trees. She led a strict life, partak-
ing of this food only once a day, but she was not so
2395 harsh with others. Nor was this daily fast of hers

without charity and prayer, for though she placed
heavy burdens on herself, she always remembered her
former hospitality and was never without paupers to
whom she gave freely whatever she had been given for
2400 herself.

With religious care and her usual piety she always
shared her table with the needy, keeping only the herbs
for herself, and she laid out food to meet their
needs with more good cheer and greater care than if she
2405 were placing it there for herself alone. In this she remembered the one she had once served on earth, who
had once hungered and thirsted, but who now no
longer needed her good offices. She remembered that
it was his will that he be refreshed in the persons of the
2410 poor. The handmaid of Christ recalled what Christ had
said of his own: 'That which you do for the least of my
people, you do for me.' For this reason, as she once had
ministered to the head of the Church, so now she provided for the members of Christ, always showing love
2415 and kindness to all. And because God loves a cheerful
giver, he gave his handmaid his merciful comfort, and
so that an inexhaustible fountain might rise up in new
plenty, the faithful, out of devotion, always gave her
the means to replenish her storehouse, which she emp-
2420 tied of everything every day in works of mercy. For with
her inborn liberality, she gave gladly. Even the rich,
who streamed to her in great numbers, she did not send
away empty: they always carried back something
good for their souls or bodies.
2425 Her clothing, made of sackcloth, was rough. For
seven years she wore tightly bound to her flesh a girdle
of horsehair full of knots, until her flesh became putrid
and worm-infested. Oh incomparable patience — that
even while living in the flesh she let her flesh be food
2430 for worms! Her feet were always bare, and her head

covered with a veil [*tyara*] of camel's hair. For her bed
she spread down tree branches and brushwood, and she
placed a stone beneath her for a pillow. In the midst of
such delights, the most holy Martha, a thousand times
2435    a martyr, sighed in spirit for Heaven.

Her soul, given entirely to God, lost itself completely in holy prayer and night-long vigil. Tirelessly
she knelt in adoration of the one who had once been
seen in her humble house and who now reigned in
2440    heaven. Moreover, she often went into the cities and
towns preaching the faith of the Lord and Saviour to
the people, and returning to her solitude, carried back
many handfuls of believers. For what she taught with
words, she proved at once by signs and miracles. By
2445    prayer and by the imposition of her hands alone, she
cast demons out of the bodies of the possessed, drawing
all her power from the power of the Holy Spirit.

CHAPTER XLII

One day the blessed Martha sat before the gates of
Avignon, a city of the province of Vienne, in a pleasant
2450    spot between the River Rhône and the ramparts of the
city preaching the word of life to a crowd of citizens and
healing the sick. A youth on the other side of the Rhône
saw the people gathered around and wished to hear the
word of God. Though there was neither bridge nor
2455    boat by which he might cross, he was so carried away by
his desire to hear her and to see miracles that he stripped
himself to the skin, and, trusting in his skill in swim-
ming, threw himself into the Rhône and began to
swim. When all the citizens across the Rhône were
2460    casting their eyes on him, the waves of the Rhône began
to swell and seethe, and he was pulled under and
drowned. The people raised a clamor, praising the

young man's devotion and deploring his misfortune.
What more? All the people decided with one mind and

2465    one will to send fishermen with nets to search with all
their might for the body of the youth and see whether
through the mercy of the Lord and Saviour, it might be
found.

The next day, at the ninth hour, after much dif-

2470    ficult searching, they found him, and brought him up,
and called for the most holy Martha. All the citizens
gathered to see this sight. The nobles of the city, of both
sexes, begged and pleaded on their knees with the
handmaid of Christ that they might be allowed to see

2475    the might of Christ the Saviour in the resurrection of
this young man. She consented, but nonetheless she required all of them to swear to come to the christian
faith. They all shouted with one voice: 'We believe that
he who has chosen such a one as you to be his servant is

2480    the Lord and Saviour, the true Son of God, and the true
God himself!'

Filled with joy by this, the blessed Martha,
trusting in the faith and power of the Lord and Saviour,
prostrated herself in tears and prayed, and the people,

2485    moved by this, also prostrated themselves, and with
great wailing begged mercy of Almighty God that he
would deign to show his power in this miracle to the
honor and glory of his name. Her prayer completed,
the handmaid of Christ got up and went to the boy.

2490    'Young man,' she said, 'in the name of our Lord and
Saviour Jesus Christ, arise and tell us what great things
the mercy of the Redeemer has done for you.'

Why keep you in suspense? Summoned by her
voice, the spirit returned and the youth was revived;

2495    and he sat up, and at once confessed that he believed in
Christ, and was baptized, and after much rejoicing and
praising with the people, he returned safe and sound to

his own home. Seeing this, the people shouted all together: 'Jesus Christ is the true God and there is no 2500   other God before Christ our God.'

From then on, the fame of Martha, the most holy servant of Christ, was on the lips of all; from then on, she was beloved by men and honored by women.

## CHAPTER XLIII

Soon after this, the news of this great deed began 2505   to spread throughout all the provinces of Gaul, and especially through Vienne and Narbonne and Aquitaine, like the odor of a field which the Lord has blessed, and it moved the souls of all the people of the province to the faith of Christ and the love of the servant of Christ, 2510   Saint Martha. Her sister, Mary Magdalene, who must be named with utmost reverence, rejoiced with her and congratulated her. Her protector and guide in her most holy life of contemplation, the archbishop Maximinus, whose soul was inflamed with the desire to see and to 2515   speak with the servant of Christ, journeyed to Tarascon from his diocese, the second Narbonnaise in the province of Vienne. Likewise, Archbishop Trophimus from the city of Arles and Bishop Eutropius from Orange came to Tarascon with the same intent, and 2520   will, and desire. And though none of them knew of the coming of the others, they all arrived on the same day at the same hour, each of them equally inspired by God, who disposes all things graciously.

The holy woman received them with honor, served 2525   them with liberality, and held them there tenaciously. And on the sixteenth kalends of January, which is the seventeenth day of the month of Kislev, which is called December among the Latins, they dedicated as a church of the Lord and Saviour the house of the blessed

2530 Martha, made famous by miracles and by her holy life.
After the dedication of the church, the most holy Martha served the bishops with due affection as they feasted.

2535 Many others had also gathered there, and the wine was running out. So the hostess of the Lord and Saviour commanded that water be drawn up in the name of Jesus Christ and served to all the guests abundantly. When the bishops tasted it, they saw that the water had been changed into the finest wine. And because of this,

2540 they commanded, in a common decree, that that day be honored every year in commemoration of the dedication of the church and the miraculous changing of the water into wine.

CHAPTER XLIV

After the death of blessed Martha, the custom

2545 arose, on the occasion of this miracle, of celebrating the feast of her passing, together with that of the passion of Saint Lazarus the bishop, her brother, on the day of the dedication of her house. We see the same thing practiced to this day with regard to the blessed John the

2550 Baptist and the apostles of Christ, John and James, Simon [the Zealot] and Jude, and a great number of other martyrs. That is to say, their passions are celebrated not on the day on which they suffered, but on the day on which their churches were dedicated or

2555 on which their relics were found.
Then the blessed bishops, bidding farewell to the handmaid of Christ, commended themselves to her most holy merits and prayers, and having given mutual benedictions, they went their own ways. The blessed

2560 woman sent a greeting to her venerable and universally acclaimed sister, Mary Magdalene, and begged her in-

sistently to consent to visit her while she was still alive. When the blessed lover of God learned this from the archbishop, she returned her sister's greeting and pro-
2565    mised to grant her request, which promise she fulfilled, though not while she was alive, but after death. From this we learn that the saints of God remember their own and fulfill after death what they promise in the flesh.

At about this time there arose in the province of
2570    Aquitaine a savage persecution among the gentiles, and many Christians were thrust into exile. Among them were Fronto, bishop of Périgueux and George, [bishop of] Vetula, who fled to Tarascon to the blessed Martha. She received them under the sign of holy chari-
2575    ty, and entertained them magnificently, and kept them in all honor until it became possible for them to return to their own dioceses. When they were leaving for their own churches, the handmaid of Christ, by way of her last farewell, said: 'Oh bishop of Périgueux,
2580    know that in this next year I shall finish this pilgrimage of mortal flesh. I pray your Holiness if you please to come back and bury me.' To this the bishop replied: 'God willing, oh daughter, I shall come to your funeral rites, if I am still alive.' Then the bishops returned to
2585    their dioceses.

Calling her own to her, the blessed Martha foretold to them the day of her passing in the coming year, and for the space of that entire year she lay in all her nobility on her bed of brushwood, consumed by a
2590    fever as gold is refined in the furnace.

CHAPTER XLV

Meanwhile, the blessed Mary Magdalene devoted herself to heavenly contemplation and kept the best part which she had chosen. Although in the flesh she

still walked in this earthly pilgrimage, she was nonethe-
2595  less permitted to walk in spirit amid the delights of
Paradise, on whose ineffable sweetness she feasted as
much as is possible for a mortal. But who can describe
how the friend of the Saviour drew out her life in sighs
of longing, even though she often enjoyed the com-
2600  pany of angels? Truly, I say, she burned with desire,
wanting to be with Christ and to see him reigning in
majesty as before she had seen him in the humble form
of a servant.

At last the time drew near when her most holy soul
2605  would depart from her body and enter that court for
which it fainted and longed, that it might be more
firmly joined to its Lord. The Son of God, the Lord and
Saviour, appeared to her, and she saw him—Jesus
Christ, her only desire—with a multitude of angels call-
2610  ing her to himself lovingly and mercifully: 'Come my
beloved, and I shall place you on my throne, for the
king desires your beauty, more lovely than any of the
sons of men. Receive the reward of heavenly life from
him whom you served so faithfully while he was on
2615  earth conversing with men. Rejoice and exult forever
amidst the heavenly choirs.'

At last the special friend of the Lord and the apostle of the Saviour passed out of this life on the eleventh
kalends of August. Amidst the rejoicing of angels, she
2620  was made one of the company of heavenly Virtues, and
was judged worthy to enjoy with them the brightness of
eternal glory and to behold the King of Ages in his
beauty. The blessed bishop Maximinus embalmed her
holy body with diverse spices and placed it in a wonder-
2625  ful tomb. Later he built a grand basilica [*honorifice ar-
chitecturae . . . basilicam*] over her blessed remains.
On her tomb, which is made of white marble, can be
seen in sculpture a representation of the scene in the

2630 house of Simon in which she was promised forgiveness
of her sins, together with a depiction of the services she
rendered to the Lord for his burial.

CHAPTER XLVI

While these things were happening in Aix, the
metropolis of the [second] ecclesiastical province of
Narbonne, Martha, the holy servant of the Lord and
2635 Saviour, lay on her bed in Tarascon in the province of
Vienne, wasting away with fever but nonetheless praising God. In the midst of her heavenly meditation, she
saw a choir of angels bearing the soul of her sister Mary
Magdalene into heaven. She summoned those who
2640 were attending on her and told them what she had
seen, and asked them to rejoice with her. And she exclaimed: 'Oh most beautiful sister, what is it that you
have done? Why have you not visited me as you promised and swore to do? Are you then going to enjoy
2645 without me the embraces of the Lord Jesus, whom we
both love so much and who loves us so much? Wheresoever you go, I shall go also. In the meantime, you will
indeed live the life eternal and grow strong in endless
bliss, and mindful of your soul, you shall not be veiled
2650 in forgetfulness.'
Then the holy woman, enraptured by this vision,
desired more than ever to die and be with Christ. It was
bitter for her to remain any longer in the flesh, and be
deprived of the company of her sister and of the angels
2655 she had seen. And knowing that the time of her passing
was close, she admonished the faithful and taught them
and comforted them, for the news of the approaching
death of the handmaid of Christ could not be kept
quiet, and a great multitude of the faithful had
2660 gathered. So that they might remain with her until she

was buried, they pitched tents in the fields and built
fires everywhere.

### CHAPTER XLVII

On the evening of the seventh day following, she
commanded that seven candles and three lamps be lit.
2665 And about the middle of the night, when everyone was
in a deep sleep, having been worn out with watching,
suddenly a great blast of wind extinguished all the
candles and lamps. Seeing this, the handmaid of
Christ, making the sign of the cross, prayed against the
2670 snares of the demons. Then she aroused her servants
and asked them to rekindle the lights. They ran to
fulfill this order but were delayed for a while. And,
behold, a sudden light shone down from heaven and in
that light appeared Mary Magdalene, the apostle of
2675 Christ, the Lord and Saviour, carrying in her right hand
a burning torch with which she immediately lit the
seven candles and three lamps that had been extinguished. Then she stood by her sister's bed and said:
'Hail, holy sister.' And in reply to her sister's return
2680 greeting, she added: 'I have come to visit you while you
still live in the flesh as you made me promise through
the blessed bishop Maximinus. And your beloved, the
Lord and Saviour, is also here and calls you from this
vale of misery, just as he appeared to me before my
2685 passing and led me into the brightness of his palace.
Therefore, come, and do not delay.'
      She spoke, and then ran joyfully to the Lord, who
entered, and drew near, and looked on Martha with a
serene face, and said: 'Behold, here I am, to whom you
2690 once ministered with great devotion out of your own
means; to whom you showed a most gracious hospitality; for whom you have done many good deeds since

my Passion in the persons of my people; to whom you
once said, prostrated in reverence: "I believe you are the
2695     Christ, the Son of the Living God who has come into
this world." Come, then, my hostess, come out of your
exile. Come, and you shall receive your crown.'

Hearing this, she raised herself and struggled to
get up and follow the Saviour at once. He said to her:
2700     'Wait, for I go to prepare a place for you, and I shall
return again and take you to myself, that where I am
you may also be with me.' Having spoken, he disappeared, and her sister Saint Mary also vanished, but the
light in which they had appeared still remained. Then
2705     the servants returned and were amazed to find the
lights which they had left behind extinguished now
throwing out an extraordinary light.

CHAPTER XLVIII

When the day came, she commanded them to
take her outside. Even the greatest haste seemed slow to
2710     her, and that morning seemed to be a thousand years
long. They set her pallet under a shade tree and on the
pallet they placed a hairshirt on which they drew a cross
with a cinder. And when the sun rose, the handmaid of
Christ was brought out and at her request candles and
2715     an image of the crucified Saviour were placed before
her face. After resting peacefully for a little while, she
looked on the multitude of the faithful and asked them
to pray that her passing might be hastened. When they
began to weep, she cast her eyes to heaven and said:
2720     'Oh you who were my guest, oh Lord Saviour, why do
you delay? When shall I come and appear before your
face? Since you spoke to me at daybreak, my soul faints
within me. Since that moment, all my limbs have lost
their motion, my nerves are paralyzed, my bones

2725 melted, my marrow cracked, and all my innards dried
up. Lord, do not disappoint me of my hope. My God,
do not tarry. My God, do not delay.'
In the midst of this meditation, she remembered
she had once seen how Christ on the cross expired at the
2730 ninth hour, as it is told in the story of Christ's passion,
written in the Hebrew tongue, that she brought with
her out of Jerusalem. And she called Saint Parmenas by
name and asked him to read that story to her to ease the
weariness of waiting. Nor did things turn out otherwise
2735 than she hoped, for when she heard read to her in her
own language the sufferings of her well-beloved, she
burst out in tears of compassion and began to weep,
forgetting for the time being her own death in fixing
all her attention on the passion story. When she heard
2740 how Christ had commended his spirit into the Father's
hands and died, she sighed deeply and expired. She fell
asleep in the Lord on the fourth kalends of August,
eight days after the passing of her sister Saint Mary
Magdalene, on the sixth day of the week at the ninth
2745 hour of the day, in the sixty-fifth year of her life.
Her body was embalmed with appropriate honor,
and enshrouded, and carried into her own church by
the companions who had come with her from the East
and remained attached to her to that very day. They
2750 were Saint Parmenas, together with Germanus, and
Sosthenes and Epaphras (who were comrades of Saint
Trophimus, archbishop of Arles), and also Marcella,
her servant, and Euchodia and Syntex. These seven
kept a three-day vigil in her honor, together with a
2755 multitude of people who came from all around and
who sang praises to God around the holy body until the
third day, lighting candles in the church, and lamps in
the houses, and fires in the fields.

CHAPTER XLIX

On the day of the sabbath they prepared for her
an honorable sepulture in her own church which the
bishops had dedicated. On that day, which is rightly
called the Lord's Day, at the third hour of the day, all
the congregation gathered to bury the holy body in a
fitting manner. This was on the first kalends of August.
And behold, at that same hour in Périgueux, a city of
Aquitaine, the bishop Fronto fell asleep in the cathedral
while the people were waiting for him to celebrate
mass. Christ appeared to him and said: 'My son, go and
fulfill what you promised. Celebrate the funeral rites of
my hostess Martha.'

He spoke, and at once — as though in the winking
of an eye — they appeared in Tarascon, in the church,
holding books in their hands, Christ standing at the
head and the bishop at the feet of the body, which they
alone placed in the tomb, to the astonishment of the
people gathered there. When the funeral was over,
they came out. One of the clerics followed them and
asked the Lord who he was and where he came from.
The Lord said nothing, but gave him the book he was
holding. The cleric went into the tomb again, and
showed the book to the crowd, and read this on one of
the pages: 'The memory of Martha, the hostess of Christ,
will be eternal; she shall have nothing to fear from evil
tongues.' The book contained nothing else.

Meanwhile, in Périgueux, a deacon awoke the
bishop, whispering that the hour of the sacrifice had
passed and the people were getting tired. The bishop
said to him: 'Do not trouble yourself or weary yourself
with waiting any longer. I have just been taken in spirit
— though whether in the body or out of the body I do
not know, God knows — to Tarascon with the Lord and
Saviour to bury the body of his servant, the holy Mar-

2760

2765

2770

2775

2780

2785

2790

tha, as I promised her when she was still alive.
Therefore, send someone to bring back my ring and my
2795  gloves, which I left in the hands of the sacristan while I
was placing the holy body in the tomb.'

Hearing this, the people were amazed and sent
messengers to Tarascon. The people of Tarascon wrote
to the people of Périgueux concerning the day and hour
2800  of the burial, which were unknown to the latter. They
said that they had seen the venerable bishop, whom
they knew well, at the funeral with another person, and
they also told of the book and its inscription, to see if
the bishop knew anything about it. Finally, they
2805  returned the ring which the sacristan had received
together with the gloves, which the people of Périgueux preserved as a testimony to this great miracle.

Some of those who had ministered to the servant
of the Saviour returned to the East to preach the King-
2810  dom of God. They included Epaphras, Saint Marcella,
and the blessed Syntex, who sleeps in a tomb at Philippi, as the apostle relates. The blessed Syntex rested at
last, and Parmenas, full of faith and pleasing to God,
won the glory of martyrdom. Germanus and Euchodia
2815  worked at comforting the faithful and were helpers to
the apostles, along with Saint Clement and other colleagues whose names are written in the book of life.

Miracles without number occurred in the church
of the blessed Martha from the day of her falling asleep.
2820  The blind, the deaf, the mute, the lame, the paralytic,
the withered, the lepers, the demoniacs, and others
stricken with various illnesses received healing. Clovis,
king of the Franks and Teutons, who first [of these na-
tions] received the marks of christian faith went to
2825  Tarascon, moved by the number and magnitude of the
most blessed Martha's miracles, and, as soon as he had
touched the tomb of the saint, was delivered of a grave
sickness of the kidneys which had tormented him

miserably. In witness to such power, he gave to God all
2830    the land within three leagues of the Church of the most
holy Martha on both sides of the Rhône, along with the
towns, villages, and forests, and he confirmed the deed
with his seal. To the present day, the holy woman
possesses this in perpetual immunity. Thieves, free-
2835    booters [*rapinae*], those who commit sacrilege, and
false witnesses find there the sudden judgement of
God and swift and horrible punishment, to the praise
of the Lord and Saviour.

### CHAPTER L

It is enough that we have told the deeds, the holy
2840    life, and the precious death of the most holy Martha,
the venerable servant of the Son of God, the Lord and
Saviour. We reserve for another work the story of the
miracles that occurred after her passing, and also the account of the virtuous life and passion of her brother,
2845    the blessed Lazarus, bishop and martyr. We shall take
care only to refer briefly to the miracles performed by
the lover of God, Mary Magdalene, first touching briefly on the passing of the holy archbishop Maximinus.
Seeing the time coming when he should be taken
2850    up out of this light to receive from the holy judge the
reward of his labor (all this having been revealed to him
by the Holy Spirit), the most holy Maximinus commanded that the place of his burial be prepared in the
church which he had built with such splendor over the
2855    holy relics of the blessed Mary Magdalene, as we have
told above. He ordered that his tomb be placed near
the sarcophagus of the blessed Mary Magdalene, the
lover of God. After his holy passing, when the faithful
had buried his holy body with honor, this place was

2860 graced by the power of the many miracles worked
through the intercession of both saints for the welfare
of the souls and bodies of those who prayed to them.
The place afterwards became so holy that no king,
prince, or other person, no matter what earthly pomp
2865 attended him, would enter the church to pray for help
without making some sign of humble devotion, first
disposing of his weapons and all other marks of brutal
ferocity. No woman was ever so audacious as to enter
that temple, no matter what condition, order, or digni-
2870 ty she enjoyed. That monastery is called the Abbey of
Saint Maximin, and was built in the county of Aix, and
is provided with all things belonging to honor.

The blessed bishop Maximinus passed into heaven
and was joyously crowned on the sixth ides of June.

# COMMENTARY:

## EXPLANATORY AND CONTEXTUAL NOTES

*lines* 3-14. *Mary Magdalene . . . Syrian.* Saint Jerome, *Liber de nominibus hebraicis,* interprets the name *Mary* as 'bitter sea' or 'star of the sea' and *Magdalene* as 'of the tower' (CC 72: 137, 144, 152). *Martha* he glosses as 'angry' or 'provoking' (CC 72: 141). The sense is that she angers and provokes the devil by her good life. *Lazarus,* says Jerome, means 'helper' (CC 72: 140). Most legends identify Mary's father as a certain Cyrus (var. Syrus), a reading that perhaps originates in a confusion of his name with his legendary homeland, Syria. According to Jerome, *Theophilus* means 'lifting up', 'converting', or 'beloved of God' (CC 72: 149). No gloss is given for *Eucharia,* though it surely must come from the Greek for 'thanksgiving'.

25-33. *Genius thrived . . . honesty.* With this description of the talents and accomplishments of the three siblings, and with the description of Saint Martha in ll. 45-55 below, cf. Vincent of Beauvais, *Speculum historiale* in *Bibliotheca Mvndi sev Specvli Maioris.* 4 vols. (Douai: Baltazar Belleri, 1624; rpt. photag. fac., Graz Austria: Akademische Druck- und Verlagsanstalt, 1964-1965) IV: 355 (hereafter cited as *Speculum historiale*). Of Saint Martha, Vincent says: 'From her childhood, she loved God greatly, was learned in Hebrew letters, obedient to the precepts of the Law, beautiful in body, attractive in face, brilliant in eloquence, and skilled in all tasks appertaining to women. Excelling all other women in piety, overflowing with charity, thriving in chastity, she avoided all contact with men. Nowhere do we read that she had a husband . . . Possessed of an abundance of wealth and full of good service and probity, she distributed to her household and family their necessities with a free hand, and was famous for

117

her hospitality, and greatly skilled in the preparation of feasts.' Vincent continues with a discussion of her charity to strangers.

60–61. *a mixture . . . lillies.* 'The delightful colors white and red become even more delightful in combination. They set each other off to achieve the fullness of beauty. The radiant white makes the red stand out, the red makes the white more intense. Whiteness brings charm, redness joy, to the perfection of loveliness. Indeed, without a dash of red, whiteness verges on pallor; and red unmixed with white inclines to the sombre. Thus, each is a good color, but in conjunction they are especially good, above all in him [the Bridegroom in the Song of Songs] who is the highest goodness, uniquely beautiful.' (John of Ford, *SC* 4.1; CF 29: 111; CCCM 17: 55). John distinguishes four whitenesses and four kinds of red. The first whiteness, that of milk, signifies untried innocence; the second whiteness, that of lillies, signifies chastity; the third, the whiteness of snow, represents penitence; and the fourth, the whiteness of light, represents holiness and is 'not of this age'. (Sermon 3. 2–5; CF 29: 99–109; CCCM 17: 49–54). The four types of red are the red of vermillion (penitential shame), of rose (virginal modesty), of blood (justice), and of ruby (burning love). (Sermon 4.2; CF 29:114: CCCM 17:56).

76. *Tarnished was . . . gold.* Of the scriptural verse (Lm 4:1) from which this passage draws, Saint Bernard says: 'The gold laments that it has grown dim, but it is still gold; its pure color is faded, but the base of the color is not altered. The simplicity of the soul remains unshaken in its fundamental being, but it is not seen because it is covered by the disguise of human deception, pretense, and hypocrisy.' (SC 82.II; CF 40: 172–173; SBOp 2: 293). Sin defaces but does not destroy the image of God in the soul, of which gold is a symbol. Cf. William

of Saint Thierry (Cant 66; CF 6:53; PL 180:494) on sin as the assumption of 'the colors of strange images'.

90–99. *But why . . . grace.* Cf. the story of the prodigal son, Lk 15:11–32. William of Saint Thierry (Cant 3: CF 6:5; PL 180: 474) uses the same imagery to discuss the call to repentance: 'Set love free in us, O Lord, that your Bride, the Christian soul, dowered with your blood and possessed of the pledge of your Spirit, may love you chastely and sing you her love songs amid the grievous sufferings of this life, in the weariness of her pilgrimage far from you and her prolonged sojourn in a strange land. Then may she be refreshed and find her pain lightened. May she be drawn to cleave to you and in the meantime forget where she is. May she hear something whereby she may understand what is wanting to her.'

102–106. *his work . . . die.* Cf. a similar gloss on the passage from Isaiah in John of Ford, SC, Sermon 27.2; CF 39: 174: CCCM 17: 222: 'After all, what is more alien to saving power than to be weak? Nevertheless, to bring us salvation, the Wisdom of God, whose foresight controls all that is, cleverly fashioned this alien work into his own, that is, into a divine work. He worked on it with nimble artistry, and he brought it powerfully to a conclusion.'

138–343. *In the . . . evil.* The stages of the Magdalen's conversion and the imagery used to describe them have many parallels in cistercian exegesis. Of particular note are the images describing the state of sin as exile, estrangement from self, and perversion of the gifts of nature and grace. The need for confidence in approaching God for forgiveness is also a favorite cistercian theme, as are a preoccupation with the wonderful effects of contact with the Word and a great interest in the action of prevenient grace. A few representative quotations illustrate the similarities.

On the perversion of natural gifts, estrangement from self, and the salvific action of the Word, Saint Bernard says: 'There is a great natural gift within us, and if it is not allowed full play the rest of our nature will go to ruin, as though it were being eaten away by the rust of decay. This would be an insult to its Creator. This is why God, its Creator, desires the divine glory and nobility to be always preserved in the soul, so that it may have within itself that by which it may always be admonished by the Word, either to stay with him or to return to him if it has strayed. It does not stray by changing its place or by walking, but it strays—as is the nature of a spiritual substance, in its affections, or rather its defections, and it degenerates and becomes unlike itself when it becomes unlike him in its depravity of life and manners; but this unlikeness is not the destruction of its nature but a defect, for the natural goodness is increased as much by comparison with itself as it is spoiled by communication with evil. So the soul returns and is converted to the Word to be reformed by him and conformed to him.' (SC 83.2; CF 40:181–182; SBOp 2:299). On the need for confidence, Bernard writes: 'Do you seek the light when you are only fit to be hidden, and run to the Bridegroom when you are more deserving of blows than embraces . . . Happy the person who hears his soul replying to these reproaches, "I do not fear, because I love; and I could not love at all if I were not loved; therefore this is love." One who is loved has nothing to fear. Let those fear who do not love; they must always live in fear of retribution. Since I love, I cannot doubt that I am loved, any more than I can doubt that I love. Nor can I fear to look on his face, since I have sensed his tenderness. In what have I known it? In this—not only has he sought me as I am, but he has shown me tenderness, and caused me to seek him with confidence. How can I not respond to him when he seeks me, since I respond to him in tenderness? How can he be angry with me for seeking him, when he overlooked the contempt I showed for him? He will not drive away someone who seeks him, when he sought someone who spurned him. The spirit of the Word is gentle, and brings me gentle greetings, speaking to me persuasively of the zeal and desire of the Word . . .' (Sermon 84.6; pp. 192–193; SBOp 2; 305–306.)

Bernard, speaking of prevenient grace, declares: "The soul seeks the Word, but has been first sought by the Word. Otherwise, when she had gone away from the Word, or been cast out, she would not turn back to look upon the good she had left unless she were sought by the Word. For if a soul is left to herself she is like a wandering spirit which does not return. . . . If a soul desires to return and asks to be sought, I would not say that it was entirely dishonored and abandoned. Whence does it obtain this desire? If I am not mistaken, it is the result of the soul being already sought and visited. . . ." (Sermon 84.3; p. 190; SBOp 2:304.

John of Ford specifically relates these images and concepts to the penitent woman who anointed Christ: 'Then there was the woman who came with an alabaster vase of ointment. Perhaps the lips of Jesus did not speak audibly to her, but deep within her heart they were distilling their dew, and she came to him bathed in it interiorly. She came looking for him who had first come to her, she anointed him who had before anointed her, and she laid hold of him who had laid hold of her in the first place.' (SC, Sermon 23.4. CF 39:120–121; CCCM 17: 196).

159. *possessed of seven demons.* An identification of these seven demons as the seven deadly sins early becomes a commonplace in christian scriptural exegesis.

179. *Blush to see.* Blushing, says John of Ford, removes the tarnish of sin (see note to l. 76 above), restoring the radiance of holiness to the face of the sinner: "How precious is this red that covers the whole countenance and makes it ruddy

with shame and radiant with holiness. . . . The red of this shame is good, able to temper the former look of the discolored face and to restore my inborn radiance. . . . Then what of the fact that we see the very appearance of our books brightened by this color, and the important letters used as chapter headings usually outlined in it? Clearly, the page of our whole behavior will be silent and unsightly, especially to the eyes of the inward reader, unless animated by the vivid color of this shame.' (SC, Sermon 4.4). CF 29: 115–116; CCCM 17: 56–57. See also the note to ll. 60–61 above.

193. *south wind.* Gilbert of Hoyland develops the symbolism of the north and south winds at length in SC, Sermons 38.1–7 and 39.1–6; CF 26: 457–474; PL 184:198–207. The two winds take turns blowing on and through the 'gardens' of the Church or of the soul, bringing different 'seasons' in a natural and proper order. The north wind signifies adversity, persecution, 'heretical tempest', trial, 'inner anxiety and boredom', and a variety of other temptations in the contemplative life. The south wind represents prosperity in the Church, consolation, joy, and grace. The north wind is also associated with Christ's tomb and the sorrow of Holy Saturday, whereas the south wind is associated with the resurrection, with Pentecost, and with the 'wind' of the Spirit. The north wind is bondage under the Old Law; the south wind, liberty under the New Law. The 'perfumes' of virtue are 'chilled and congealed' by the north wind, but spread abroad by the south wind. Whereas the north wind 'binds' and 'restrains', the south wind 'loosens' and 'replenishes'. Gilbert tells his audience that when '[you] spread your wings to the south wind and grow feathers for the flight to heaven', the north wind will try to 'intervene and with freezing blast to check the new growth of your wings', but assures it that although this wind 'does hamper your wings from flight' it

'does not blow your wings away'.

The VBMM's use of this imagery seems to suggest that Mary, having endured the north wind of penance, is now ready for the southerly wind that brings growth in the religious life.

280–284. *Then, turning . . . serenity.* John of Ford sees the eyes and glances of Jesus as symbols of the operation of grace: 'To look at those eyes is to have received a promise of grace; to be looked at by them in turn is to have received grace itself, here and now. In a word, nobody is holy, nobody is or can be good if he has not found grace in those eyes. Those eyes are full of grace, or, better put, they are themselves the fulness of grace, because a look from them suffices for every inpouring or confirming of grace in the sons of grace.' (SC, Sermon 19.1; CF 39: 60–61; CCCM 17:165). Christ's long gaze at Mary and his finding a reflection of himself in her eyes is a sign that Mary's conversion is complete.

305. *for she . . . much.* See also ll 756–757 below. Saint Bernard applies these words, from Lk 7:47, to the Bride in the Song of Songs and to the Church. (SC Sermon 14.7.; CF 4:103; SBOp 1:80).

363–390. *He cured . . . love.* See Lk 8:43–48 and parallels. Lines 366–390 of this passage are quoted from Eusebius, *Ecclesiastical History* (ed. H.J. Lawler, trans. K. Lake and J.E.L. Oulton, 2 vols. [London and New York: William Heinem, Ltd. and E.P. Putnam's Sons, 1926–1932], II:175–176. The latin translation in PG 20: 679–680 of Valesius' seventeenth-century edition does not correspond very closely to the Latin of VBMM.) Rufinus of Aquileia (345–410) translated Eusebius in nine books around 402. Modern editions follow a ten-book division.

The Martha legend in *Legenda aurea* also relates the story of the statue, noting that Ambrose thought the woman was Saint Martha herself, and that Saint Jerome and *Historia Tripartita* tell how Julian the Apostate substituted his own image for that of Christ. The image was struck by thunder and broken in pieces. See Jacobus de Voragine, *Legenda aurea*, ed. T. Graesse (Leipzig, 1846) p. 444, or F.S. Ellis' modernization of Caxton's translation (London: Dent, 1900) IV: 138. Caxton takes the word '*Emorroissa*' as the woman's name. In the Magdalen legend, both Jacobus and Caxton accept the identification as Martha.

Jacobus' allusion to Ambrose is probably based on a spurious work. A note to the sermons of Peter Chrysologus (PL 52:296, n. f) refers to a 'pseudo-Ambrosian' sermon presented as number 48 in the appendix to a 'new edition of Ambrose' (probably that of Ballerini: Milan, 1875–1886) which holds that the woman stricken by the flux and Saint Martha are the same. This sermon was probably Jacobus' authority. The *Historia Tripartita* is a compilation of extracts from the writings of Sozomen, Socrates of Constantinople (Socrates Historian), and Theodoret Lector. These writers continued Eusebius' history up to their own times. Epiphanius, under the direction of Cassiodorus, made the extracts and translated the Greek into Latin. For the passage in *Historia Tripartita* to which Jacobus alludes, see PL 69:1052–1058. I have not been able to find the material in Jerome's works.

Besides Martha of Caesaria Phillippi and Saint Martha, there is another woman sometimes identified as the *haemorissa*. The apocryphal *Gospel of Nicodemus* gives the name 'Veronica' to the woman, perhaps intending to identify her with the famous Saint Veronica whose cloth received the imprint of Christ's face when she wiped the sweat from it. See *The Gospel of Nicodemus*, ed. H.C. Kim (Toronto: Centre for Medieval Studies, 1973) p. 22. For a Middle English version of the work, see W.H. Hulme, ed., *The Middle English Harrowing of Hell and Gospel of Nicodemus* (London: Trübner, 1907).

Gilbert of Hoyland interprets the woman's disease as "that flow of carnal attraction, of carnal licentiousness and anxiety" which the presence of Christ and the mere touch of his garment banish. (SC 1.2; CF 14:45; PL 184:13). John of Ford uses the story of Christ's healing of the woman to illustrate the medicinal power of the fringes of the Spouse's robe, praised by the Bride in the Song of Songs. (SC 36.2; CF 43:86; CCCM 17:271–272).

The *Glossa Ordinaria* (PL 114: 276) sees the *haemorissa* as a type of the gentiles: 'This woman touched the hem of his garment, coming to him in faith and believing in him devoutly, knowing wisely that she would be cured. Just so, the people of the gentiles who believed in God, who repented and left off their sins, who espoused the faith and believed, showing their devotion as they were called, knew wisely' where to find health. Rabanus Maurus, *De Universo* (PL 111: 76) sees her as a type of the Synagogue, which when cleansed by Christ, becomes the Church.

412–413. *feasting with . . . contemplation.* For the image of contemplation as feasting, see also ll. 281–282 above. Gilbert of Hoyland uses this image in SC 11.3; CF 14:143; PL 184:59. For John of Ford, the culmination of the contemplative life is the marriage feast of the Bride and Bridegroom (SC 43.5–6; CF 43:159–160; CCCM 17:311).

413–414. *'I sit . . . beloved.'* VBMM alludes to this again at ll. 1623–1624. John of Ford interprets the shadow of the beloved as the shadow of the tree of life, which, like St Peter's shadow (Ac 5:14–15) can heal, and which offers protection from temptation. (SC 38.7; CF 43:112–113; CCCM 17:288). Both allusions to the verse in VBMM occur in the context of Christ's defense of Mary against the complaints of Martha, suggesting that the protectiveness of the beloved's shadow is being invoked, perhaps against mistaken criticisms of the contemplative life.

435–437. *Joanna, whose . . . Galilee.* Joanna, according to Lk 8:3, was the wife of Chuza, steward to Herod Antipas.

468–496. *'Who is . . . souls.'* Another example of this imagery of conception and motherhood appears in ll. 227–229 above. For excellent discussions of the motherhood image in twelfth-century spiritual writings, see Caroline Walker Bynum, *Jesus as Mother: Studies in the Spirituality of the High Middle Ages* (Berkeley, Los Angeles, and London: University of California Press, 1982) 110–169, and 'Maternal Imagery in Twelfth-Century Cistercian Writing,' in *Noble Piety and Reformed Monasticism,* Studies in Medieval Cistercian History VII; CS 65, ed. E. Rozanne Elder (Kalamazoo, 1981) 68–80, and Marsha L. Dutton, 'Christ Our Mother: Aelred's Iconography for Contemplative Union' in *Goad and Nail:* Studies in Medieval Cistercian History X; CS 84, ed. E. Rozanne Elder. (Kalamazoo; 1985) 21–45.

Hearing, preaching, spiritual 'conception', and 'motherhood' form a nexus of imagery in cistercian writings. Romans 10:17 — 'Faith comes from hearing' — seems to be one scriptural text responsible for the association of these things. Saint Bernard was particularly fond of expounding the Romans text; see, for examples, SC 28.5–7 (CF 7:92–94; SBOp 1:195–197); Sermon 41.2 (CF 7: 205; SBOp 2:29), and Sermon 53:2 (CF 31:59–60; SBOp 2:96–97). Since faith comes from hearing, preaching is the vehicle by which faith is instilled, and since faith leads to rebirth, instilling faith is a kind of birth-giving. The preacher is therefore a mother of souls. As John of Ford, SC 26.5; CF 39:164; CCCM 17:217, puts it: 'The name "mother" or "bride" may be applied quite justly to anyone who is moved by motherly affection to bring forth and train sons for God . . .' Saint Bernard, SC 85.13; CF 40:209; SBOp 1: 315–316, explains in greater detail: 'Spiritual persons, like holy mothers, may bring souls to birth by preaching, or may give birth to spiritual insights by meditation. . . . The soul is affected in one way when it is made fruitful by the Word, in another when it enjoys the Word. . . .' The preacher or spiritual person is not only the mother of souls, but also the mother of Jesus, since faith is the same thing as the presence of Christ in the soul. Thus John of Ford speaks of spiritual persons as both 'brides' and 'mothers' of Jesus (SC 7.2; CF 29:151; CCCM 17:74). The imagery appears repeatedly in John's series on the canticle; e.g. Sermon 19.7–8 (CF 39, pp. 70–73; CCCM 17, pp. 170–171), Sermon 26.7 (CF 39: 168–169; CCCM 17:219), Sermon 33 (CF 43.8: 56–57; CCCM 17: 259–260), Sermon 44.10 (CF 43: 176; CCCM 17:319), and Sermon 46–8–9 (CF 43: 200–201; CCCM 17: 331). Gilbert of Hoyland also employs it in his series: SC 10.3 (CF 14: 137; PL 184: 57), Sermon 24.2–3 (CF 20: 298–301; PL 184: 125–127), Sermon 43.1 (CF 26: 516; PL 184: 225), *et passim*. For other citations from these and other Cistercians, see Bynum, 'Material Imagery'. The tradition that the Virgin conceived Christ through her ear perhaps reinforces the exegete's enthusiasm for the motif. Be that as it may, Saint Bernard uses the motif of the preacher as mother to touch on such complicated issues as the relation of human actions to God's action. Though the Spirit can sow the seed of faith in the soul directly, God nevertheless allows human beings to share in this redeeming work: 'Nevertheless, there are boundless and countless achievements that he [God] carried through by means of his subject creatures, whether corporeal or spiritual, but he uses them as master rather than as suppliant. For example, he now employs my tongue for his purpose of instructing you, when he could certainly impart the same knowledge directly with greater facility on his part and more pleasure for you. This mode of acting that he has chosen represents an indulgence on his part, not indigence. He makes this promotion of your welfare an occasion of merit in me; it does not mean that he needs my assistance.' (SC 5.9.; CF 4: 30; SBOp 1: 25). With this passage, cf. VBMM, ll. 796–788 and the note to those lines.) Despite this high estimation of preaching and preachers, however, William of Saint Thierry cautions that God and not the human agent possesses the true power of generation: 'In a word, charity is poured forth in our hearts not by the teaching of man but by the Holy Spirit who is given to us. And no word, whatever its source, is effective unless the power of prevenient grace is operative in it.' (Cant 203; CF 6: 162–163; PL 180:546).

The images of the gestation and birth of faith in the writers cited above bear comparison with the concept of the gestation of obedience in the writings of another Cistercian, Garnier de Langres (var. of Rochefort). In his sermon on the feast of Saint Bernard (*Sermones,* Number 29; PL 205: 755–759), Garnier comments on Jn 12: 1–8 at length, developing an interpretation in which the home of Mary, Martha, and Lazarus in Bethany (glossed after the standard allegorical etymology as 'house of obedience') is seen as a kind of mother in which the seed of Martha's active works and Mary's contemplation, impregnated by the Holy Spirit, brings forth obedience. The gestation of obedience in the house of Simon the Leper, where Mary anointed Christ, is connected typologically to Jacob's impregnation of Rachael and Leah, who are, like Mary and Martha, figures of contemplation and active works. This impregnation brings forth the people of Israel, the nation called to obedience under the Law. Morally, the gestation of obedience also occurs in the individual soul. Simon the Leper learns humility in bearing with his leprosy.

When he becomes 'perfect' in humility and obedience, he is cured. His house then becomes a fit place for the Christ to sleep and feast. Indeed, it becomes a figure of the obedient conscience: *'sic igitur et pascit in domo Simonis, id est in conscientia obedientis.'*

499. *the breasts . . . charity.'* The allusion to the breasts of hope and charity probably draws on the extensive amount of existing commentary on the imagery of breasts in the Song of Songs. (Sg 1:13, 4:5, 7:3, 7:7–8, 8:10.)

Saint Bernard interprets the words of the Canticle in three ways: as referring to the Bridegroom, to the Bride, and to the Bride's companions. As the Bride's praise of the breasts of the Bridegroom, the verses point to the 'twofold sweetness' of Christ — his 'tireless expectancy' and 'prompt forgiveness'. As the Bridegroom's praise of the breasts of the Bride, they suggest analogies between the swelling breasts of a pregnant woman and the spiritual fecundity of one who has accepted grace: 'For so great is the potency of that holy kiss [of the Bridegroom, i.e., of grace] that no sooner has the bride received it than she conceives and her breasts grow rounded with the fruitfulness of conception, bearing witness, as it were, with this milky abundance. Men with an urge to frequent prayer will have experience of what I say. Often enough when we approach the altar to pray our hearts are dry and lukewarm. But if we persevere, there comes an unexpected infusion of grace, our breast expands as it were, and our interior is filled with an overflowing love; and if somebody should press upon it then, this milk of sweet fecundity would gush forth in streaming richness.' As the words of the Bride's companions, the verses are a plea that the Bride leave off contemplation to share her spiritual riches: 'But the breasts with which you may feed the offspring of your womb are preferable to, that is, they are more essential than, the wine of contemplation . . . Rachel may be more beautiful, but Lia is more fruitful. So beware of lingering amid the kisses of contemplation, better the breasts that flow in the preaching of God's word.' In another sermon, Bernard assigns two sligtly different meanings to the breasts of the Bride. They signify two different 'affective movements': 'compassion' and 'joyful sympathy': 'consolation' and 'encouragenent'. Elsewhere, Bernard applies the words about the Bride's breasts to the Church. See SC 9.4–10; and 10.1–2; CF 4: 55–60 and 61–62; SBOp 1: 43–48 and 48–50. See also Sermon 12.11; CF 4:86; SBOp 1: 67–68.

William of Saint Thierry, apparently inspired by Bernard's reading, offers a somewhat simpler interpretation. With reference to the Bridegroom, the breasts signify the two Testaments of the Bible; with reference to the Bride, they signify 'wisdom' and 'knowledge'. See Cant 38–39, 46, 83 (CF 6: 30–31, 36–37, and 68–69; PL 180: 485–486, 488, and 501–502).

Like Bernard, Gilbert of Hoyland speaks of the breasts of consolation, and like William, he compares the two breasts to the two Testaments. Gilbert extends this last comparison, appealing to Saint Paul's practice of adapting his minstry and preaching to his audience. Paul ministered to both Jews and Gentiles, to those under the Law and to those outside it. To fulfill this calling, he needed two different breasts with two different kinds of milk for two different kinds of children. Indeed, says Gilbert, Paul 'seems to abound in as many breasts as are the ways in which with ingenious art he adapted himself to the capacity of the weak'. Gilbert also develops an elaborate analogy between different breasts and different offices of authority. There are two breasts of 'maternal piety', he begins: "Take one of these to be the left, the other the right: the left, assistance in temporal affairs; the right, in spiritual consolation.' Kings and princes have only the left breast of temporal assistance; priests and teachers, only the right breast of consolation. Abbots and other monastic authorities, however, need both. Speaking of the beauty of these breasts, Gilbert offers an extended and rather startling comparison; 'And if you wish to hear some spiritual and more developed interpretation of their beauty, I refer you to the devices of women, who cultivate and develop physical beauty and have mastered this art. For what are they more anxious to avoid in embellishing the bosom than that the breasts be overgrown or shapeless and flabby, or occupy the spaces of the bosom itself? Therefore they constrain overgrown and flabby breasts with brassieres, artfully remedying the shortcomings of nature. Beautiful indeed are breasts which are slightly prominent and are moderately distended; neither raised too much nor level with the bosom, as if pressed back but not pressed down, gently restrained but not hanging loose. Following this model, let him who must utter good words, consoling words, imitate the art and care of women. Let him adopt restrained language; let not the breasts of his words be sloppy or tumble out in disorder. Let them not replace rather than adorn, as it were, the bosom and consistory of the mind. Let them not have more bulk than grace, more flesh than milk. Let his discourse be pure and prudent, as occasion demands. Here let piety approach and observe the rhythm of beauty. Let the discourse not have more in the mouth than in the breast, lest the milk be spilt. The breasts should rise from the bosom and cling there; the bosom should not be merged into the breasts. From the abundance of the heart let the mouth speak; let it speak from that abundance, not emptying itself entirely. The breasts must be restrained lest they spill over in excess.' (SC 27.1–5, 30–9, 31.2–4; CF 20: 329–335, 370, 375–378; PL 184:139–143, 160, 161–163.

John of Ford is less extravagant than Gilbert. He speaks of

the maternal breasts of the Incarnate Word—the breasts of 'goodness' and 'loving kindness'. Those breasts are withdrawn for a time while Christ is in the tomb, and at the Resurrection they are replaced with 'solid food—unleavened bread and a paschal lamb'. (SC 17.6–7 and 19.8–9; CF 39: 36–39, 72–75; CCCM 17, 151–153, 171–172).

509–512. *Oh truly . . . fed!* Cf. Vincent of Beauvais, *Speculum historiale,* p. 355. Vincent's passage refers only to Martha, not to all three siblings: 'O truly happy, she who merited such a guest; who fed on the bread of Angels. She received that great guest who is the receiver and pastor of men and angels.'

516–579. *In this . . . more.'* As Faillon's notes suggest, the presentation of Christ's judgment seems to be inspired by Saint Augustine, *In Johannis Evangelium,* Tractatus 33.4–6 (CC 36: 307–309), perhaps transmitted through Bede, Alcuin, or Rabanus, whose texts of the relevant passages are virtually indistinguishable from Augustine's. Often the resemblance between VBMM and Augustine or the possible intermediaries goes beyond a correspondence in thought to verbal echoing, though the verbal parallels are seldom precise.

539–579. *Bending over . . . more.'* Aelred of Rievaulx interprets Christ's writing in the dirt less elaborately, as a sign of the 'earthliness' of the accusers. Like the author of VBMM, Aelred commends this episode from scripture not only as a moral example for judges but also as an occasion for the meditation on the loving kindness of Jesus, instructing the anchoresses for whom he writes his *Rule:* 'Then call to mind the woman who was taken in adultery and what Jesus did and said when he was asked to give sentence. For he wrote on the earth, in order to show them up as of the earth rather than of heaven, and then said; "Let him among you who is without sin be the first to throw a stone at her." But when the words struck them all with terror and drove them out of the temple imagine how kind were his eyes as he turned to her, how gentle and tender was the voice with which he pronounced his sentence of absolution. Think how she would have sighed, how she would have wept as he said; "Has no one condemned you, woman? Neither shall I condemn you".' (*Inst incl* 31; CF 2: 83; PL 32: 1467).

580–762. *It was . . . sent me?* The chapters on the raising of Lazarus are heavily indebted to Saint Augustine, *In Johannis Evangelium*, Tractatus 49.4–23 (CC 36: 421–431) or to the possible intermediaries, Bede, *In S. Joannis Evangelium Expositio*, XI (PL 92: 775–781), and Alcuin, *Commentaria in S. Joannis Evangelium*, V.XXVII (PL 100: 896–903). The VBMM speeds the narrative and heightens the emphasis on the affective elements of the Augustinian material by omitting Augustine's reading of Lazarus as a type of the habitual sinner (the only such omission VBMM shares with Bede and Alcuin), the discussion of other scriptural passages that Augustine sees as pointing to similiar morals that the Lazarus story points to, the extended comment on sleep as a figure of death in scriptural language, and the glossing of the significance of the four days that pass and of the putrifaction of Lazarus' body. VBMM's description of the progress of Lazarus' illness and the pathos of the funeral, the comment on the greatness of Thomas' love, and the words about the tears of Jesus have been added to the Augustinian material. Notes below cite some of the more striking parallels between VBMM and Augustine or the intermediaries, drawing from Faillon's notes, independently verified.

581. *month of Kislev.* Latin: *Casleu.* Third month of the Hebrew calendar.

716–717. *Jesus, whom . . . will.* Cf. Augustine, *In Johannis Evangelium*, Tractatus 60.2 (CC 36:479).

735–736. *most holy . . . eyes.* John of Ford had a special

devotion to the holiness and beauty of the eyes of Jesus, on which he comments in SC 16.5 and 18.1–6 (CF 39:21, 46–54; CCCM 17: 143, 157–162). In the latter he says: 'In Daniel, the eyes of the son of man are compared to flames of fire and they are described by Jacob as more beautiful than wine . . . The eyes of Jesus are a gift of this twofold grace, the spirit of wisdom and the spirit of understanding.'

744–745. *He could . . . sick.* Cf. Augustine, *In Johannis Evangelium* Tractatus. 19.5 (CC 36:190).

762–810. *Having said . . . him.* The discussion of Jesus' crying out and the association of the raising of Lazarus with confession and sacerdotal absolution may be at least remotely indebted to Augustine, *In Johannis Evangelium,* Tractatus 22.7 (CC 36:227): 'The Lord cried out at the sepulchre of Lazarus, and he that was four days dead arose. He who stank in the grave came forth into the air. He was buried, a stone was laid over him: the voice of the Saviour burst asunder the hardness of the stone; and thy heart is so hard, that that Divine Voice does not yet break it! Rise in thy heart; go forth from thy tomb. For thou wast lying dead in thy heart as in a tomb, and pressed down by the weight of evil habit as by a stone. Rise, and go forth. What is Rise, and go forth? Believe and confess. For he that has believed has risen; he that confesses is gone forth. Why said we that he who confesses is gone forth? Because he was hid before confessing; but when he does confess, he goes forth from darkness to light. And after he has confessed, what is said to the servants? What was said beside the corpse of Lazarus? "Loose him, and let him go." How? As it was said to His servants the apostles, "What things ye shall loose on earth, shall be loosed in heaven."' Translation by John Gibb and James Innes, *Homilies on the Gospel of John,* in *A Select Library of the Nicene and Post-Nicene Fathers,* Vol. 7 (NY, 1888, rpt. Grand Rapids: Eerdmans, 1956) p. 147.

792. *the just Joseph.* Joseph of Arimathea (see Lk 23:50) is probably intended, but Joseph Barsabbas, surnamed Justus, whom the apostles rejected as the replacement for Judas Iscariot in favor of Matthias (Ac 1: 23), is another possibility.

793. *that blessed man.* The righteous rich man of the Book of Ecclesiasticus (Sirach). See Si 31: 9.

796–798. *On the . . . does.* In his treatise, *On Grace and Free Choice,* (CF 19: 51–111; SBOp 3: 196–198), Saint Bernard repeatedly addresses the problem of God's use of human agents to achieve divine purposes. Bernard carefully says that God needs no human assistance but that he often graciously allows human beings to participate in his work, and that when the human being cooperates willingly, the merit is real and not merely token: 'For when God, our King from of old, worked salvation in the midst of the earth, he divided the gifts which he gave to men into merits and rewards, in order that, on the one hand, our merits might be our own here and now by free possession, and, on the other, by a gracious promise, we might await their recompense as our due. . . . If David spoke truly when he said: "There is none that does good, except one" — that one, namely, of whom it is also said: "No one is good but God alone" — then both our works and his rewards are undoubtedly God's gifts, and he who placed himself in our debt by his gifts constituted us by our works real deservers. To form a basis for such meriting he deigns to make use of the ministry of creatures, not that he stands in any need of it, but that through this or by its means he may benefit them . . . For God truly communicates the work he carries out through them to those who consent in will to what they do in act. . . . God, therefore, kindly gives man the credit, as often as he deigns to perform some good act through him and with him.' (CF 19.43–45: 100–104; SBOp 3: 196–198.)

829–833. *He who . . . day.* Augustine, *In Johannis Evangelium,* Tractatus 9.6; CC36: 93–99, identifies the six ages as: from Adam to Noah, from Noah to Abraham, from Abraham to David, from David to the Exile, from the Exile to John the Baptist, and from John the Baptist to the end of the world. He gives an extended discussion in the remainder of the tract (9.6–16; CC 36: 93–99). In Tractate 117.1–2 (CC 36: 651–652) Augustine attempts to harmonize different scriptural accounts regarding the hour in which Christ was crucified. Faillon notes similar typologies in Alcuin and Rabanus.

    839–841. *Lazarus was . . . ghost.* Cf. Augustine, *In Johannis Evangelium,* Tractatus 50.5. (CC 36:435.)

    848–851. *That ointment . . . eyes.* Adulterated perfumes and deceitful perfume-makers are particularly noisome to cistercian exegetes of the Song of Songs. Gilbert of Hoyland, glossing the text, 'Like pure balsam is my fragrance,' (Si 24: 21), distinguishes three degrees of spiritual perfection or lack thereof, all symbolized by ointments of varying purity: 'There is then, to enumerate: balsam which is genuine and unadulterated; balsam which although genuine is adulterated; balsam which is neither genuine nor unadulterated. The first is found in the perfect, the last in those who are deceived; the central balsam in those who although not deluded by any fallacy, lack the grace of some virtue.' (SC 17.5; CF 20:223; PL 184: 90). Later in the same sermon, Gilbert includes Mary Magdalene, along with the companion Marys, Nicodemus, and Saint Paul, among those who can procure genuine balsam; that is, who can be guides in the 'discernment of spirits', in the interpretation of spiritual states of being. (SC 17.6 CF 20:224; PL 184: 91.) The insistence on the purity of the Magdalen's ointment suggests the fulness of grace she has received and the degree of spiritual perfection she has reached.

    852. *nard.* In a mystical sense, according to Rabanus Maurus, *De universo* (PL 111: 527–528), nard symbolizes the 'odor of sanctity' in the Church. Nard and crocus are associated

with the waters of baptism. Cyprum, an aromatic extract of the cyprus tree, signifies the grace of heavenly benediction; nard signifies the passion of Christ; crocus, the fervor of charity. Cyprum also signifies incorruption; nard, fortitude; crocus, martyrdom. Saint Bernard, glossing the text, 'While the king was on his couch, my nard gave forth its fragrance' (Sg 1: 11), interprets nard as representing devout humility: 'The nard is an insignificant herb, said by those who specialize in the study of plants to be of a warm nature. Hence it seems to be fittingly taken in this place for the virtue of humility, but aglow with the warmth of holy love.' For Bernard, this reading applies particularly to the humility of the Virgin. (SC 42.5–11; CF 7: 214–219; SBOp 2: 36–40). William of Saint Thierry appropriates Bernard's reading, but applies the symbolism to the Magdalen, invoking the story of her anointing of Christ: 'Spikenard is a low-growing herb, with abundant foliage and ears; it is the symbol of humility, fruitful in virtues. It is hot, signifying the heat of holy desire. It is good for the making of perfumes, because in God's sight there is no loving devotion without the virtue of humility. It has an excellent odor — signifying, in humility, the confession of sins. We see this in the alabaster jar of genuine nard or precious ointment, which the humble devotion of a woman poured upon Jesus's body, ɩ ɪointing it in advance for burial. Hence concerning the fragrance of the humble nard, that is, of devout confession, the Gospel adds: "And the house was filled with the odor of the ointment."' (Cant 77; CF 6:65; PL 180: 499–500) For Gilbert of Hoyland (SC 36.3–5; CF 26: 439–440; PL 184: 190), nard is the peace of mind that is a 'prerequisite' for contemplative vision. Gilbert associates the herb with Christ's repose in the tomb that precedes the glorious vision of the resurrection. See also Sermon 32.7; CF 20:392–393; PL 184: 170, for a direct application of the nard symbolism to Mary

Magdalene.

877. *a fire . . . love.* See also line 1193 and 1370. In VBMM, the fire of love is a common image, as it is in many medieval spiritual writings, the *Incendium Amoris* of the fourteenth-century english mystic Richard Rolle being only one of the more noteworthy examples. (See Clifton Wolters, trans., *The Fire of Love* [Penguin, 1972]). The author of VBMM invokes the image at moments of special intimacy between Mary Magdalene and Christ. St Bernard, speaking of the transforming power of this fire, also links its operation with the nurturing presence of God, with the condition that it work under God's illuminating scrutiny: 'Furthermore, when this fire has consumed every stain of sin and the rust of evil habits, when the conscience has been cleansed and tranquilized and there follows an immediate and unaccustomed expansion of the mind, an infusion of light that illuminates the intellect to understand Scripture and comprehend the mysteries — the first given for our own satisfaction, the second for the instruction of our neighbor — all this undoubtedly means that his eye beholds you, nurturing your uprightness as a light and your integrity as the noonday . . .' (SC 57.8; CF 31: 102–103; SBOp 2: 124). The career of Mary Magdalene as presented in VBMM follows the pattern Bernard traces: purgation from sin and redemption of conscience, followed by the acquisition of peace and the illumination of the mind, both culminating in witness.

915–916. *the demon . . . midday.* In SC 33.9; CF 7: 152–153; SBOp 1: 239–240, Saint Bernard provides a clue for why Judas is here associated with the noontide demon of Ps 90:6 (Hebr 91: 6). This demon, like Judas, covers his wickedness with a mask of righteousness, hoping to snare the unwary: 'For we cannot defend ourselves from the attack of the noontide devil except with the aid of noontide light. I believe he is styled the noontide devil because some of those wicked spirits, who, because of their obstinate and darkened wills are like the night, even perpetual night, yet, for the purpose of deceiving men, can become bright as day, even as noon. . . . Hence when this kind of noontide devil sets out to tempt a man, there is no chance whatever of parrying him; he will tempt and overthrow his victim by suggesting what appears to be good, by persuading him, unsuspecting and unprepared as he is, to commit evil under the guise of good, unless the Sun from heaven shines into his heart with noontide brightness.' Perhaps Christ's rebuke of Judas is taken to be an instance of such intervention.

952-953. *led by . . . love.* Cf. Augustine, *In Johannis Evangelium,* Tractatus 50.14 (CC 36:439)

984-996. *Going out . . . mountains.* Gilbert of Hoyland and John of Ford offer a different reading, interpreting the curse of the fig tree as Christ's displeasure with someone who displays outward marks of charity (leaves) but no inner truth (fruit). See Gilbert of Hoyland, SC 40.3; CF 26:480; PL 184: 209, and John of Ford, SC 45.6; CF 43:186; CCCM 17: 324.

1011. *fawn.* The same image from Sg 2: 9 is used at l. 1634 below. Cistercian writers comment on the image at length. To Saint Bernard, it recalls the fleetness of the Word of God in hastening to save. 'Christ is, moreover, spoken of as a fawn rather than as an adult stag to remind us that he first manifested himself in gentleness, as a child, rather than in overwhelming power.' The deer's sharpness of sight suggests the divine discernment in separating the evil from the good. Joy in the Lord is invoked in the 'caprices and gladness of the fawn'. (SC 55.1-2, 73.1-6, 74.7-8; CF 31: 82-84; CF 40: 75-80 and 92-93; SBOp 2; 111-112, 233-237, 244.) William of Saint Thierry takes substantially the same meaning, but reinforces his discussion with a somewhat more philosophical treatment of the divine nature. For William, the juxtaposition of roe and fawn or 'young hart' in the canticle suggests the dual nature of Christ. The roe represents his divinity; the young hart, his humanity. (Cant 152–153; CF 6:124–125; PL 180 528–529). Gilbert of Hoyland sees the fawn or 'young hind' imagery as an allegory of the spiritual, contemplative life. With the 'alacrity' and 'nimbleness' of the young hind, a spiritual person transcends his earthly life and fleshly temptations to scale the heights of the religious life. The 'longevity' of the hind is also significant, for it suggests renewal: 'Hinds are said to preserve themselves from old age by a natural ability and by a vivifying renewal to summon from dissolution a life in decline. Christ in a special way is described not as a hind but as a young hind; he relies on eternal youth and has no ingredient of age which might later require renewal.' Finally, the sure-footedness of the hind suggests the ability to search out the Spirit in rough and hidden places: 'That is why our text speaks of hinds of the fields, because anything rugged or steep is for them level and open and accessible to their unimpeded flight, like the ranges of an open plain. The voice of the Lord is the voice of intimate inspiration flowing gently into the ears of the mind. That is surely the voice which trains hinds such as these and discloses his lairs to them. For if there are any hiding places overgrown with a thick tangle of scandals as if with brambles, they are not impenetrable for those whose feet the Lord makes like the hoofs of hinds, who cannot be hindered by any harmful obstacle but rather take pleasure in hardship and are trained to accept wrongs or to take them in stride in their passionate desire to hasten to the heights and to forge ahead.' (SC 14.2–5; CF 14: 166–169; PL 184: 68–70). In an earlier sermon, Gilbert uses the skittish behavior of a fawn as a metaphor for the contemplative's experience of the seemingly arbitrary character of grace. At times one is given the grace of Christ's presence, but at other times it is withdrawn or withheld. It comes and goes; seeks and evades for reasons not always detectable. (SC 1.1; CF 14: 44; PL 184:11).

1031–1032. *The skin . . . Saviour.* VBMM may have appropriated the allusion to Jb 19:20 from Odo of Cluny's sermon on the Magdalen. Odo writes: 'And thus was accomplished in the time of the Lord's Passion what the blessed Job had once said — "My bones cleave to my flesh, and I have escaped by the skin of my teeth." For when the disciples fled, Mary Magdalene remained with the Lord, as fast as the bones cleave to the skin.' See *Acta Sanctorum,* July V: 220.

1126. *Joseph of Arimathea.* Discussions of the legend of Joseph of Arimathea appear in nearly all general treatments of the Arthurian cycle. Several short versions of the legend of Joseph in Middle English were edited by W.W. Skeat in *Joseph of Arimathie* (London: Trübner, 1871; rpt. New York: Greenwood Press, 1969). The long poem by Herry Lovelich, *The History of the Holy Grail* (1450), a translation from Middle French, was edited by F.J. Furnivall for the EETS (London: Trübner, 1874–1877; rpt. 1901) in three parts (2 vols.). In brief, the story goes that Joseph, after many trials and adventures, arrived in Wales with the Holy Grail. There he and his company were imprisoned, but they were soon freed by an English king responding to a vision sent to him by Christ. Joseph founded an abbey at Glastonbury, where he died and was buried. Many miracles were worked at his tomb. For Glastonbury, see *The Chronicle of Glastonbury Abbey: An Edition, Translation and Study of John of Glastonbury's Cronica sive Antiquitates Glastoniensis Ecclesie,* ed. James P. Carley, trans. David Townsend (Woodbridge, Suffolk: Boydel, 1985.

1207–1208. *After that . . . immortality.* The passage may owe a generalized debt to Homeric descriptions of dawn, as in *Odyssey,* II, 1–7 and III, 1–5.

1252–1253. *and two . . . Luke.* Faillon's interpolation.

1284–1287. *Here, where . . . affection.* As Faillon notes, the sentence echoes Augustine, *In Johannis Evangelium,* Tractatus 120.6 (CC 36:663).

1352–1361. *But Mary . . . sealed.* Cf. Augustine, *In Johannis Evangelium,* Tractatus 121.1 (CC 36: 664). Faillon notes corresponding passages in Bede, *In S. Joannis Evangelium Expositio,* 20 (PL 92: 913), Alcuin, *Commentaria in S. Joannis Evangelium,* 41 (PL 100: 989), and Rabanus Maurus, *Homiliae in Evangelia et Epistolas,* Homily 12 (PL 110: 160–161). The similiarities between VBMM and these authorities is remarkable but the verbal correspondence is not precise.

1361–1372. *Nevertheless . . . eyes.* Cf. Augustine, *In Johannis Evangelium,* Tractatus 121.1 (CC 36: 664): 'Was it that her grief was so excessive that she hardly thought she could believe either their eyes or her own? Or was it rather by some divine impulse that her mind led her to look within?' (Gibb and Innes, p. 437.) Bede, *In S. Joannis Evangelium Expositio,* 20 (PL 92: 918) presents a corresponding passage.

1378–1379. *as though . . . whole.* Cf. Augustine, *In Johannis Evangelium,* Tractatus 121.1 (CC 36:665). Faillon, PL 112:1472, note f, notes corresponding passages in Gregory the Great, Bede, Alcuin, and Rabanus.

1380–1382. *And this . . . sorrow.* Cf. Augustine, *In Johannis Evangelium,* Tractatus 121.1 (CC 36:665). Corresponding passages in Bede and Rabanus.

1431–1451. *'Do not . . . Father.* The explanation of why Mary is not allowed to touch the risen Christ — that her mind is not yet prepared to receive the truth of his equality with the Father — is a commonplace of scriptural exegesis.

1443-1444. *The grain . . . heart.* The figure of the mustard seed appears in the resurrection discussion of Augustine, *In Johannis Evangelium,* Tractatus 121.3 (CC 36:666) and Bede, *In S. Joannis Evangelium Expositio,* 20 (PL 92: 919). The garden (or vineyard, or orchard) of the heart and soul, with Jesus as its gardener, is a commonplace image. Saint Bernard speaks of sin as the spoiling of a vineyard which 'God, not man, had planted'. (SC 63.2; CF 31: 163; SBOp 2: 162). The verse from Sg 4: 12 — 'a garden enclosed is my sister, my bride' — is traditionally applied to the Virgin, but Gilbert of Hoyland associates it with all religious souls: 'Into this garden, good Jesus, you readily descend to the beds of spices, to recline in this garden, to be its gardener and its guardian.' The garden signifies 'interior delight'; the enclosure, 'the discipline of standing watch'. Christ cultivates the garden in two ways — by planting and by weeding; by inspiration and by discipline. These reflections lead Gilbert into a discussion of the garden of Paradise, whose first gardener, Adam, was negligent. See SC 35.1-2; CF 26: 426-428; PL 184:183-184. John of Ford presents an extended interpretation along similar lines in SC 44.8-11 and 45.1-6; CF 43: 174-186; CCCM 17:318-325.

1457-1459. *Just as . . . apostles.* See also ll. 1665-1670 below. Saint Bernard applies the words *evangelist* and *apostle* to all of the women who came to the tomb, not only to Mary Magdalene: 'Sent by the angel they did the work of an evangelist, and became the apostles of the apostles, and while they hastened in the early morning to give their news of the mercy of God, they said, "We will run in the fragrance of your perfumes".' (SC 75.8; CF 40: 104; SBOp 2: 251-52)

1486-1508. *'Behold how. . . . apostles.* The typological linking of Eve and Mary Magdalene appears in christian exegesis at least as early as Ambrose, *Expositio Evangelii secundum Lucam* (PL 15: 1936-1937).

1588. *Nicopolis . . . Palestine.* Called Emmaus in the Gospel.

1639–1665. *But without . . . . reward.* The three anointings mentioned in this passage elicited a great amount of commentary from patristic and later medieval exegetes. According to Saxer, *Le culte,* II: 328–329, 'mystical' interpretations in the manner of Saint Jerome's are typical of early patristic writers, while 'moral' interpretations in the manner of Saint Augustine's dominate later medieval exegesis. Faillon's summary of the mystical reading (*Mon. inéd.* I: 288–316) is a composite of material drawn from Gregory the Great, Bede, Eusebius Gallensis, Zacharias Chrysopolitanus, Peter Chrysologus, Cyril of Alexandria, Paulinus, Hilary of Poitiers, Theophylactus, Paschasius Robertus, Ambrose, and Rupertius. The glosses of Christianus Druthmarus, Rabanus Maurus, and the *Glossa Ordinaria* also conform to the general pattern of mystical interpretation. Faillon's summary merges the first and second anointings. The Pharisee is a type of the Jews, who do not believe in Christ's mission. Christ's entry into the Pharisee's house is his entry into the Jewish nation, the house of obedience to the Law ('Bethany' is usually glossed 'House of Obedience' and 'Simon' as 'the Obedient'). Christ's sitting down at the table is a sign of his humility in submitting himself to the Law: it is also a foreshadowing of his sacrifice. The meal is a type of the Eucharist. The sinful woman (Mary Magdalene) is a figure of the idolatrous gentiles who eventually become part of the church. Her hearing the news of Christ's arrival and her response to it show that by the preaching of the apostles, the gentiles learn that God has sent his Son as Saviour. Her coming to the feet of Christ represents the humility of the gentiles, who do not claim the special status of election through the Law. Her washing of Christ's feet with tears signifies the gentiles' recognition that Christ gave his body to redeem them. His feet represent Christ's humanity; his head represents his divinity. The drying of his feet shows how great Mary's love is; she uses as a towel what was before her most prized possession, her hair. The ceaseless kissing of Christ's feet signifies the tender love of the gentiles, which continues through all ages. The perfuming of his feet represents the preaching of the incarnation throughout the world (perfume being associated with preaching, and Christ's feet, once again, with his humanity.) In the second scene, the anointing of Christ's head represents adoration of his divinity. The alabaster box, which, on being broken, perfumes the entire house, is a figure of the evangelistic fervor of the gentiles. The perfume is a type of the martyrs. Judas, in his reproach, signifies the envy of the Jews. The Pharisee in the first anointing scene is similarly interpreted as a type of the Jews in their disdain for the gentiles, whom they consider idolatrous. The parable of the debtors is an allegory of the Jews and gentiles.

In contrast to this ecclesiological or mystical reading which sees Mary Magdalene as a type of the church of the gentiles, the moral reading interprets her as a type of the individual soul in penitence and conversion. Augustine, Anselm of Bec, Raoul Ardent, Geoffrey of Vendôme, Peter Damian, Nicholas of Clairvaux, Peter of Celle, and Peter of Blois are among the authorities Saxer cites as emphasizing this interpretation. Some authors, the Cistercian Garnier of Rochefort, for instance, develop both the mystical and moral readings. In a sermon on the Eucharist (*Sermones,* Number 16; PL 205: 677), Garnier speaks of three kinds of anointing—unction of the sick, of the catechumens, and of the newly-baptized —which correspond to Mary Magdalene, Mary Jacobi, and Mary Salome. They also correspond to the three anointings of Christ, though Garnier lists these a bit differently than most authorities do; i.e., as the anointing in the House of Simon, as the unction of Christ's crucified body, and as the unction the Father bestows on the exalted Christ in heaven. These are prefigured in the three unctions of King David—by Samuel, by the men of Judah, and by all of Israel.

Other cistercian exegetes developed a somewhat different symbolism of ointments and anointing in their sermon cycles on the Song of Songs. Bernard of Clairvaux, speaking of the ointments on the breasts of the Bride (SC 10–12; CF 4: 63–85; SBOp 1: 50–67), mentions the ointments of contrition, of devotion, and of piety or loving kindness: 'The first is pungent, causing some pain; the second mitigates and soothes pain; the third heals the wound and rids the patient of the illness.' In explaining the first ointment, he specifically alludes to the episode of Christ's anointing in the House of Simon. Just as there the penitent woman's ointments filled the house with their sweetness, so, when a sinner repents, the whole Church is filled with joy. This ointment is made from things available to all; one can 'cull' them from one's 'own little garden' at any time. The second ointment, however, is made of things that come from above. The 'poor', that is, those who lack faith and confidence, cannot afford the necessary ingredients for the second kind of ointment. The first ointment is applied to Christ's feet, representing human things; the second, to his head, representing divine things. The third ointment, the ointment of loving kindness, is so called because its ingredients consist of 'the needs of the poor, the anxieties of the oppressed, the worries of those who are sad, the sins of wrong-doers, and finally, the manifold misfortunes of all classes', to which those who possess the ointment minister. Bernard mentions Saint Paul, Joseph (son of Jacob), and King David as examples, and says that the ointments of the Magdalen at Christ's tomb were of this kind also, since they were meant for Christ's entire body, from head to foot, thereby encompassing both his humanity and his divinity. Bernard is not sure that Mary Magdalene is the same person as the woman who had the other two ointments, but sees a progression in the three instances of anointing nonetheless.

Thus, through the symbolism of ointment, the Magdalen and the Bride are linked. As Marjorie Malvern, *Venus in Sackcloth: The Magdalen's Origins and Metamorphoses* (Carbondale: Southern Illinois University Press, 1975) 62–65 and 82–85, notes, Bernard's views originate in Origen's exegesis of the Canticle.

The action of anointing possesses a similar richness of suggestion for Cistercians. Gilbert of Hoyland (SC 33.8; CF 26: 407; PL 184: 176) says: 'To sum up in brief: anointing is an exultation of the mind and its fragrance is prayer. Anointing is spiritual gladness and its fragrance is some exterior awareness by reputation of what takes place in the spirit. Anointing is inward delight and its fragrance is a desire flowing gently from joyful experience.' He then links anointing more specifically with the act of contemplation: 'Therefore "the fragrance of your ointments surpasses all perfumes". Indeed the incense of every other prayer and desire is surpassed in vehemence by that longing which is born from the wooing of heavenly joy and from the ardor, which like a most enchanting fragrance, rises in abundance from the anointing of the Spirit.' With a similar association of anointing and contemplation, Aelred of Rievaulx describes spiritual exercises in terms of the Magdalen's various actions the three times she anointed Christ (*Inst incl* 31; CF 2: 83–86; PL 32: 1467–1468.)

1671–1688. *Mary Magdalene's . . . relieved.* With this passage, cf. Saint Bernard: 'It was perhaps for this reason the Lord Jesus would not allow the mixture of spices to be used on his dead body, he wished to reserve it for his living body. For that Church which eats the living bread which has come down from heaven is alive: she is the more precious Body of Christ that was not to taste death's bitterness, whereas every Christian knows that his other body did suffer death. His will is that she be anointed, that she be cared for, that her sick members be restored to health with remedies that are the fruit of diligence. It was for her that he withheld these precious ointments, when, anticipating the hour and hastening the glory of his resurrection, he eluded the women's devout purpose only to give it new direction. Mercy and not contempt was the reason for this refusal; the service was not spurned but postponed that others might benefit. And the benefit I refer to is not the fruit of the material thing, this anointing of the body; it is a spiritual benefit symbolized by it. On this occasion he who is the teacher of religious devotion refused these choice ointments that are symbols of devotion, because it was his absolute wish that they be used for the spiritual and corporal welfare of his needy members.' (SC 12.6–7; CF 4: 82–83; SBOp 1)

1716–1729. *But most . . . God.* With this encomium on souls who take the Magdalen as pattern, cf. Saint Bernard's gloss on the ointments of contrition, consolation, and loving kindness: 'Happy the mind that has been wise enough to enrich and adorn itself with an assortment of spices such as these, pouring upon them the oil of mercy and warming them with the fire of charity! Who in your opinion, is the good man who takes pity and lends, who is disposed to compassionate, quick to render assistance, who believes that there is more happiness in giving than in receiving, who easily forgives but is not easily angered, who will never seek to be avenged, and will in all things take thought for his neighbor's needs as if they were his own? Whoever you may be, if your soul is thus disposed, if you are saturated with the dew of mercy, overflowing with affectionate kindness, making yourself all things to all men yet pricing your deeds like something discarded in order to be ever and everywhere ready to supply to others what they need, in a word, so dead to yourself that you live only for others — if this be you, then you obviously and happily posses the third and best of all ointments and your

hands have dripped with liquid myrrh that is utterly enchanting.'
(SC 12.1, CF 4:77–78; SBOp 1:)

    1725–1729. *Such a . . . God.* Cf. William of Saint Thierry,
Cant 94 CF 6:76–77; PL 180: 505–506: 'When humble love turns
toward God more ardently, it is conformed to him toward whom
it turns; because as it turns it is given by him an aptitude for such
conformity. And since man is made in the likeness of his Maker,
he becomes attracted to God; that is, he becomes one spirit with
God . . . He is then in God, by grace, what God is by
nature . . . But in the vision of God, where love alone is
operative without the cooperation of any other sense, in a manner
incomparably nobler and more refined than any imagination due
to the senses, purity of love and the divine attraction play this
same role . . . they transform the faithful lover wholly, mind and
activity, into God, not only strengthening him, but conforming
him and vivifying him that he may have fruition.'

    1869–1919. *Truly amid . . . embraces.* The sorrow Mary
feels when she loses the presence of Christ is a repeated theme in
VBMM (see, for example, ll 1352–1361 above) and is comparable
to the theme of contemplative desolation so dear to cistercian exegetes of the Canticle. Since the contemplative life aims at enjoy-
ing the immediate fellowship of God, a sense of abandonment is
particularly devastating to some pursuing that life. William of
Saint Thierry's description of the vicissitudes of contemplation is
representative: 'The affection and entire life of these souls are
divided between grief and joy—grief for the absence of the
Bridegroom and joy at his presence; and their one hope is the eternal joy of the vision of him. And they experience this not once nor
in one manner, but often and in many different manners. All this
laborious but holy exercise in the heart of the lover [that is, the life
of the proficient] is the affair not of a single day but of con-
siderable time; it is manifold and varied, following the devotion

of the soul's different attractions and the course of its spiritual progress.' Cant 32 CF 6: 26–27; PL 180: 484.

1873–1878. *It is . . . parting.* With this passage, cf. Bernard, SC 26.10, lamenting the death of Gerald of Clairvaux: 'It is but human and necessary that we respond to our friends with feeling: that we be happy in their company, disappointed in their absence. Social intercourse, especially between friends, cannot be purposeless; the reluctance to part and the yearning for each other when separated, indicate how meaningful their mutual love must be when they are together,' (CF 7: 69; SBOp 1: 178). A comparison of the Latin texts (relevant passage in VBMM, PL 112: 1485–1486) shows clear verbal borrowings.

1973–1974. *They were . . . Nicholas.* Ac 6: 5. The martyrology of Rabanus Maurus (PL 110: 1121–1188) omits most of the seven deacons. However, Rabanus' contemporaries— Ado, Florus, and Usuard—list feasts for all but Nicholas, who may be excluded from the catalogues of saints because, according to Irenaeus and Hippolytus, he founded the heretical Nicolaitan sect mentioned in Rv 2: 6, 15. See James Hastings, ed., *Dictionary of the Bible,* rev. ed. F.C. Grant and H.H. Rowley (New York: Scribners, 1931). Feast days: Stephen, December 26; Philip, June 6; Parmenas, January 23; Timon, April 19; Prochorus, April 9; Nicanor, January 10 (all according to Usuard). Biblical authorities do not agree whether Philip the Deacon should be identified with Philip the Evangelist, mentioned in Ac 8: 5; 8: 26; 8: 40; and 21: 8–9. With the exception of Stephen and Philip the Evangelist, the deacons are omitted from *Legenda aurea* and works derived from it.

1984–1985. *frequently sharing . . . visitations.* On the angelic visitations the Magdalen experiences, see also ll 2302–2314 below. Saint Bernard declares that all prayerful contemplatives may hope to enjoy this privilege: 'The man who lives in this state habitually will have the angels for his frequent and familiar guests, especially if they frequently find him in prayer.' (SC 7.7; CF 4: 43; SBOp 1: 35).

    2019. *follow in . . . perfume.* To be drawn by or to follow in the fragrance of someone's perfume is an expression, taken from Sg1:3, routinely used to describe the emulation of another's virtue or holiness. Saint Bernard, to cite only one example, uses it in a eulogy to Saint Malachy the Irishman (CF 10: 104; SBOp 5:423): 'Let us, beloved, run to this place of refreshment, eager in spirit, in the odor of the ointments of our blessed father who we see this day to have stirred up our sluggish spirits to a burning, ardent desire.'

    2058. *sixteenth kalends of January.* December 17. This feast of the Eastern Church (which actually celebrates Martha of Bethany and her sister Mary, who in the Eastern tradition is distinguished from the Magdalen) is often listed under December 19 or January 19. After the time of Gregory the Great, the feast was not generally observed in the West, though Rabanus' martyrology does list a commemorative feast of Mary and Martha, 'the sisters of Lazarus', on January 20 (discrepancies of a day or two are not unusual in Rabanus' martyrology) and a separate feast for Mary Magdalene on July 22, the traditional Western date. This inclusion of separate feasts might seem to suggest that Rabanus follows the Eastern distinction between Mary of Bethany and Mary Magdalene, were it not for the fact that in other works he affirms the Western identification of the two women (see, for example, *De universo*, PL 111: 84). For a discussion of the Eastern and Western feasts, see Saxer, *Le culte*, I; 34–39; II: 281, 324–325, *et passim;* and *Acta Sanctorum*, July V: 16.

    2067–2069. *to which . . . apostles.* The tradition that Evodius was the first bishop of Antioch appears at least as early as Eusebius (*Chronicon*, anno 2055; *Ecclesiastical History*, III. 22). Usuard, drawing from Ado, writes under May 6: 'Saint

Evodius, who, as the blessed Ignatius writes, was ordained as
first bishop [of Antioch] by the Apostles, ended his life in the
same city by a glorious martyrdom.' (Usuard, *Martyrologium,*
in Jacques Dubois, ed., *Le Martyrologe d'Usuard* [Brussels:
Societé des Bollandists, 1965.]) Rabanus' martyrology does not
contain an entry for this feast day. W. Smith and H. Wace,
eds., *A Dictionary of Christian Biography,* 4 vols. (London:
Murray, 1877–1887) II: 428, allude to a legend that Evodius invented the term 'Christian'.

2077–2088. *In the fourteenth . . . Rome.* With this account of the *divisio apostolorum,* cf. Eusebius, *Ecclesiastical
History,* III. 1, and Vincent of Beauvais, *Speculum historiale,*
p. 344. John Beleth, *Rationale divinorum officiorum* (PL 202:
143–144), discusses a feast day honoring the event.

2100–2103. *Mary Magdalene . . . companions.* VBMM
quotes *Vita apostolica* here. (Faillon, PL 112:1491–2, notes e-g.)

2109. *Herod.* Herod Agrippa I, *d.* 44 AD.

2112–2115. *Thus, in . . . . Christ.* From *Vita apostolica*
(Faillon, PL 112: 1491–2, notes e-g.)

2130–2131. *Saint Mary . . . Maximinus.* By regulation,
female recluses had to have a recognized confessor and spiritual
director. Vincent of Beauvais, *Speculum historiale,* p. 356,
adds that not only was Maximin Mary's advisor, but that he had
also been the one who baptized Mary and Martha.

2165–2201. *To Saint . . . doctors.* The persons mentioned in ll. 2189–2193 as the companions of Saint Martha are
not included in the number of the seventeen bishops sent into
Gaul. The list of Martha's companions is composed mainly of
names that appear in the Book of Acts or the apostolic letters.
How the legend arose that these persons accompanied Saint
Martha into Gaul and later returned to the East after her death
is unknown. See ll. 2746–2753 and 2808–2817 below.

Parmenas was one of the original seven deacons.

Epaphras is mentioned in Col 2: 7–8; 4: 12–13; and Phm: 23.

He is referred to as a native of Colossae and as the 'fellow servant' and later 'fellow prisoner' of the apostle Paul. Legends recorded in the carolingian martyrologies call him the first bishop of Colossae. Feast day: July 19.

In Ac 18: 17, a certain Sosthenes is said to be the ruler of the synagogue at Corinth. Medieval legends associate him with the 'brother' in 1 Co 1: 1. Carolingian martyrologies mention him as Paul's disciple, but say nothing of a journey to Gaul. Feast day: November 28.

Germanus. No one by this name appears in the Bible, and the number of Gaulish saints with this name makes it difficult to identify the one intended here.

Euchodia (var. Euodia) and Syntex (vars. Synthyce, Syntyche) are the two women whom Paul urges to reconcile their differences in Ph 4: 2. Carolingian martyrologies say nothing of a sojourn in Gaul. Feast day (Syntex): July 22.

The ecclesiastical geography outlined in this passage conforms closely to the administrative organization of Gaul in the late Empire (*c.* 395), but not to merovingian or post-merovingian organization. See William R. Shepard, *Historical Atlas* (New York: Holt, 1928), 'The Roman Empire about 365', pp. 42–43, and the map in Olwen Brogan, *Roman Gaul* (Cambridge, Massachusetts: Harvard, 1953) 213.

The origin, development, and transmission of the legend of the seventeen bishops sent into Gaul to evangelize the region are obscure, but fragments of evidence regarding some aspects of the legend exist.

Gregory of Tours, *Historia Francorum,* I. 28, says that seven bishops were sent to Gaul: Catinus (Gatianus in VBMM) to Tours, Trophimus to Arles, Paul to Narbonne, Saturninus to Toulouse, Dionysius to Paris, Stremonius to Clermont, and Martial to Limoges. (Gregory of Tours, *History of the Franks,* 2 vols., trans. O.M. Dalton [Oxford: Clarendon, 1927], II: 20; PL 71: 175–176.) In *De gloria martyrum* (*Libri Miraculorum,* Bk. I),

Gregory includes entries for two other men listed among the seventeen in VBMM — Eutropius of Saintes (Chp. 56) and Feroncius (Ferrucion, Ferutio) (Chp. 71). Eutropius, according to Gregory, was sent by Saint Clement, not by Saint Peter. It is not clear whether Gregory distinguishes this Eutropius from Eutropius of Orange, as VBMM does, or identifies the two men, as some later authorities, including the *Legenda aurea,* do. Feroncius, says Gregory, was the companion of Saint Ferreolus. Both were martyred at Besançon. Feroncius' rank — whether he was a bishop, presbyter, or deacon — is not specified. The only other member of the seventeen mentioned in *De gloria martyrum* is Saturninus (Chp. 48), who is said to have been sent not by Saint Peter but by all the apostles in general. Gregory tells in detail the story of his martyrdom on the capitol at Toulouse. For a latin text and modern french translation, see Gregory of Tours, *Les Livres des miracles,* trans., H.L. Bordier, 4 vols. (Paris: Jules Renouard, 1859–1864) Vol. I. A latin text is also printed in PL 71: 705–800.

Closer in content to VBMM but still different in significant ways are the accounts of the martyrologists Ado, Florus, and Usuard. These authorities mention sixteen of the bishops, omitting Maximinus. Although the listing of the various ecclesiastical jurisdictions conforms to that of VBMM, the source of authority — who ordained and sent the bishops — is not always given as Saint Peter as it is in VBMM. The martyrologists claim that Saint Paul the apostle sent Paul the Bishop; the 'see of Rome' sent Gatianus; the 'apostles' sent Trophimus and the two companions, Fronto and George. Saint Irenaeus sent Feroncius as the companion of Saint Ferreolus (the latter is not mentioned in VBMM), and Feroncius is a deacon, not a bishop. According to Ado, the apostles sent Sabinianus and Potentianus; according to Usuard, 'Rome' sent them. In general, VBMM seems to be more concerned about concentrating authority in one party clearly linked to the papacy. Its foundation legend offers less ground for a province or diocese to assert any degree of autonomy on the basis of a founder who received his authority from a source rivalling the antiquity or prestige of the papacy.

Rabanus Maurus, the elder contemporary of the martyrologists discussed above, lists only six of the bishops: Valerius, Martial, Saturninus, Feroncius (as Ferrutio the Deacon, with Ferreolus), and Fronto and George. Rabanus also mentions, under August 5, the tradition that Saint Peter sent Memmius, Dionysius, Sextus, and Eucherius to evangelize Gaul, a legend that seems to contradict the legend of the seventeen.

Separate carolingian legends not associated with a martyrological collection exist for some of the seventeen. For Fronto, Martial, and Austregisilus, see Josephe-Claude Poulin, *L'idéal de Sainteté dans l'Aquitaine carolingienne* (Quebec: Les Presses de l'Université Laval, 1975), especially the bibliographies in the appendices. For Fronto, see also Maurice Coens, 'La Vie Ancienne de S. Front de Périgueux', *AB* 48 (1930) 324–360, which contains an edition of a *vita* of the saint.

The omission from all the authorities discussed above of Maximinus, who is so important in VBMM, shows that neither Rabanus nor his contemporary martyrologists knew the legend of the seventeen in quite the form in which the VBMM presents it. Perhaps the evidence outlined above permits one to suggest a process of conflation behind the creation of the legend of the seventeen involving at least two steps. (1) Various legends about the apostolic foundations of the sixteen principal gaulish dioceses were grouped into one legend about the petrine foundations of those dioceses. (2) This composite was then assimilated by the legend of the voyage to Gaul of Mary Magdalene and her companions, among whom Maximinus was particularly important. The leading role that the carolingian martyrologists assign to Trophimus or Irenaeus was transferred to Maximinus. Perhaps scribal errors resulting from a similarity between the names Ferreolus and Ferrutio (Feroncius) led to the omission of the former and the 'promotion' of the latter from deacon to bishop.

Whatever the case may be, the legend recorded in VBMM agrees in all but a few points with the account presented by Vincent of Beauvais, *Speculum historale,* p. 356. Vincent gives a list of bishops very similar to that in VBMM, but with the following exceptions: Sabinianus, Potentianus, and Valerius are omitted, the two Eutropii are clearly distinguished, and Dionysius (omitted from VBMM) is given jursidiction over all of Gaul. Of these differences, the most remarkable is that involving Dionysius. That this saint, who became identified with pseudo-Dionysius the Areopagite in the ninth century and eventually became the chief patron of France, should be left out of VBMM seems curious, for the tradition of his coming to Gaul dates from at least the time of Gregory of Tours. Perhaps, however, the VBMM author's sense of chronology is responsible for the omission. Dionysius was supposedly commissioned by Pope Saint Clement, who is listed as one of Martha's companions in VBMM. The action related in the *vita,* however, seems to take place before Clement's reign. The traditional date of Dionysius' martyrdom, AD 96, also places his period after the supposed time of the Magdalen. The inconsistency of making Dionysius their contemporary does not seem to bother Vincent, but it may have disturbed the VBMM compiler. An obvious weakness of this explanation is, however, that similar inconsistencies involving the dates of the seventeen do not worry him in the least. Perhaps some difference in political affiliations or tastes accounts for differences in treating or not treating Saint Dionysius.

2171–2172. *Gatianus, Tours . . . Lyons.* Faillon interpolates, PL 112: 1493.

2194. *which is now Normandy.* In 911, Charles the Simple ceded to Rollo, the norman leader, much of the area that later came to be called the Duchy of Normandy.

2196. *Octodure.* Modern Martiny.

2202–2206. *And here . . . faith.* Saint Torquatus and his companions are unknown to Rabanus, but they do appear in Ado, Florus, and Usuard. According to these authorities, these seven bishops were ordained by the apostles to preach the Gospel in Spain. Feast day: May 15. For the appearance of local spanish legends in carolingian legends, see B. de Gaiffier, 'Les notices hispaniques dans le martyrologe d'Usuard', *AB* 55 (1937) 269–283. The legend of the seven, which seems to contradict the legend of Saint James' evangelization of Spain, raises the same questions with regard to widely-known accounts about national patron saints as the legend of the seventeen raises. It is not immediately clear why Saint James would be left out, especially when legends (admittedly not popular until the fifteenth century) exist which associate him with the Magdalen. In one legend, Mary Magdalene, Mary Jacobi, and Mary Salome helped Saint James evangelize Spain. After they returned with him to Jerusalem and after his martyrdom, they set sail, bearing with them the head of Saint James and the bones of the Holy Innocents. They landed at a town in southeastern France, Saintes Maries de la Mer, on the route to Compostella. In the fifteenth-century, a substantial pilgrimage cult, fostered by the dynasty of Anjou, developed there around the supposed relics of Mary Jacobi and Mary Salome. See Marina Warner, *Alone of All Her Sex* (New York: Knopf, 1976) 228–229; Saxer, *Le culte,* II: 238–239; J. Charles-Roux, *Légendes de Provence* (Paris: Bloud, 1910) 71–72; and Walter Starkie, *The Road to Santiago* (New York: Dutton, 1957) 81.

2209–2212. *preaching, praying . . . God.* From *Vita apostolica* (Faillon, PL 112: 1494, note e.)

2271–2278. *The blessed . . . herself.* On the preaching of Martha, see Vincent of Beauvais, *Speculum historiale.* p. 357.

2299–2302. *an apocryphal . . . gall.* See the same hostility to 'fables' in ll 2315–2326 below. Gilbert of Hoyland is representative in his antagonism to the apocryphal stories that were often used as amplifying *exempla* in sermons. Speech, says Gilbert, should help the spiritual person ascend to God, but idle tales merely bolt the listener more firmly to earth. Preachers, who are specially charged with helping souls to God, sin greatly when they burden holy writ with triviality: 'Now the man who slips from the sublime to the ridiculous and to empty tales does not bend down [i.e., in reverence] but falls on his face. He does indeed speak in a broken voice but he does not emit a sweet incense.' Gilbert compares the vice he attacks to infraction of the rule of silence, and to another favorite target — hairsplitting philosophizing on the sacred text. See SC 36.5; CF 26: 440–441; PL 184: 191, and Sermon 16.4–5; CF 20: 208–209; PL 184:83.

2321. *the Penitent of Egypt.* Saint Mary the Egyptian. According to the legend recorded in *Legenda aurea,* she was a public prostitute in Alexandria who, after seventeen years, joined a group of pilgrims to the Holy Land. Upon arriving, she tried to enter a holy shrine but was repulsed several times by an invisible force until she prayed to the Virgin, vowing to live from then on in penitence. Her prayer answered, she entered the shrine, prayed, and received three pence, with which she bought three loaves of bread. Then she passed over the river Jordan to live for forty-seven years in penance and solitude in the desert. The three loaves sustained her through all this time. One day, however, a priest, Zozimas, who was also seeking solitude, happened upon her. Her clothes had long since rotted off her, and her body was burnt black by the sun. Seeing Zozimas, she fled, but he followed her, not knowing what kind of creature she was. At length she asked him for his mantle and on receiving it, prayed to God and was elevated into the air as she prayed. Zozimas at first thought she was an evil spirit but on hearing her story, learnt otherwise. He promised to bring her the sacrament on Easter morning. On that day, Mary crossed over the Jordan on foot by the aid of the sign of the cross and received communion. She made Zozimas promise to return in a year's time. But when he returned, he found her dead and a note beside her body asking him to bury her. Because of the hardness of the ground, however, he could not do so until a lion came by and helped scoop out a grave. See Jacobus de Voragine, *Legenda aurea,* ed. T. Graesse (Dresden, 1846) 247–249; trans. Granger Ryan and Helmut Rippergar, *The Golden Legend of Jacobus de Voragine* (London: Longmans, 1941) 228–230. [See Benedicta Ward, *The Harlots of the Desert,* Cistercian Studies Series, 106 (Kalamazoo, 1987).]

The account of the Egyptian's desert solitude was assimilated into the Western Church's legend of Mary Magdalene well before the eleventh century. Benedicta Ward, *Miracles and the Medieval Mind* (Philadelphia: University of Pennsylvania Press, 1982) p. 260, n. 65, believes that Dominic of Evesham is responsible for the introduction. The earliest surviving greek account, Ward notes, is Cyril of Scythopolis, *Life of Cyriacus.* In Usuard, the Egyptian's feast day is April 2.

2336–2344. *terrible dragon . . . evil odor.* Jacobus gives a more graphic description of the dragon as half beast and half fish, winged, with a lion's head and a serpent's tail. The creature came from Galicia and was the offspring of Leviathan and 'Bonacho' or 'Onacho'. (Graesse, p. 444.) *Taras* and *Tauriskos* are the variants of the dragon's name (see Charles-Roux, p. 95). According to Nostradamus, the comtesse de Die, a provençal poetress who flourished in the twelfth century, composed a poem about Tarascus, *Lo Tractat de la Tharasca,* now lost. See the Benedictine Congregation of Saint-Maur, *Histoire littéraire de la France,* Vol. 15 (Paris: Palmé, 1869) 446–447. See also Vincent of Beauvais, *Speculum historiale,* p. 358.

2357–2359. *With the . . . neck.* A common method of pacifying dragons. Cf. the legend of Saint George, in which the saint subdues the beast by casting a virgin's girdle around its neck. Saint Bernard of Menthon introduces a variant — throwing a stole rather than a girdle over the dragon of the Alps. See E. Cobham Brewer, *A Dicionary of Miracles* (Philadelphia: Lippencott, 1934) 111, and Brewer's index. Martha's companion, Saint Fronto, is also said to have slain a dragon. See Brewer, p. 112.

Sabine Baring-Gould, writing in 1898, notes that the story of Saint Martha and the dragon was celebrated in Tarascon until the late nineteenth century 'by a procession of mummers, attended by the clergy, who paraded the town escorting the figure of a dragon, made of canvas, and wielding a heavy beam of wood for a tail, to the immanent danger of the legs of all who approached. The dragon was conducted by a girl in white and blue, who led it by her girdle of blue silk, and when the dragon was especially unruly, dashed holy water over it. The ceremony was attended by numerous practical jokes, and led to acts of violence, in consequence of which it has been suppressed. The effigy of the dragon now reposes in the lumber room of the theatre.' (*Lives of the Saints,* 16 vols. [London: Nimmo, 1897–1898], VIII; 625, n. 1.) Provençal tradition attributes the establishment of these *'jeux de la Tarasque'* to King René d'Anjou, about the year 1469. See Charles-Roux, p. 94, and Albert Lecoy de la March, *Le Roi René,* 2 vols. (Paris, 1875; rpt. Geneva: Slatkine Reprints, 1969), II: 137–138, 141.

2375. *Black Hearth.* Latin: *niger focus.* Jacobus calls the place *Nerluc, id est niger locus* (var. *lacus*) (Graesse, p. 444). On the origin of the name 'Tarascon', Brewer, p. 115. remarks: 'According to Greek mythology, the place received its name from *Taras,* son of Neptune'.

2387–2388. *And she . . . herself.* W.M. Metcalfe alludes to a tradition that credits Martha with establishing the first convent and first monastery in Gaul at Tarascon. See W.M. Metcalfe, ed., *Legends of the Saints in the Scottish Dialect of the*

*Fourteenth Century*, 3 vols. (Edinburgh and London: Blackwood and Sons, 1896–1897) III: 199.

2388–2389. *she proceeded . . . miracles.* At Tarascon miracles were attributed to Saint Martha well into the seventeenth century. In 1639 a fire threatened to destroy the whole town, but just as it drew near the relics, the story goes, it was miraculously extinguished. Martha is also credited with saving the town from the plagues of 1629, 1639, 1640, and 1649, and from the flooding of the Rhône many times. She is said to be not only the patron of the town but also its 'mother': '*non solum ipsorum Patrona, sed gratiosiori titulo Mater pientissima*'. See *Acta Sanctorum*, July II: 20.

2415–2424. *And because . . . bodies.* 'The man who is wise,' writes Saint Bernard, 'will see his life as more like a reservoir than a canal. The canal simultaneously pours out what it receives; the reservoir retains the water till it is filled, then discharges the overflow without loss to itself . . . Charity never lacks what is her own, all that she needs for her own security. Not alone does she have it, she abounds with it. She wants this abundance for herself that she may share it with all; and she reserves enough for herself so that she disappoints nobody. For charity is perfect only when full.' (SC 18.3; CF 4: 134–135; SBOp 1: 104–105).

2425–2435. *Her clothing . . . heaven.* With this account of Saint Martha's austerities, compare the closely similar account in Vincent of Beauvais, *Speculum historiale*, p. 358.

2448–2503. *One day . . . women.* Jacobus' account of this miracle omits the mass conversion. Baring-Gould notes that the story was included in the 'ancient' offices commemorating Saint Martha in Avignon, Tarascon, and Autun. He also writes that: 'A chapel stands on the spot where the miracle is said to have taken place, in the street of Vielles Lices, and is called Calade.' (VIII: 626.) See also Vincent of Beauvais, *Speculum historiale*, p. 358.

2507. *like the . . . blessed.* Gn 27: 27. For Gilbert of Hoyland, the line suggests bountifulness (SC 15.2; CF 14: 179; PL 184: 74–75). For John of Ford, it suggests the perception of the coming of grace from afar (SC 20.2; CF 39: 79; CCCM 17: 174). The odor of the field, says John, arouses the soul to the love of God.

2512–2543. *Her protector . . . wine.* Jacobus' legend of Martha omits the story of the bishops' visit and the changing of water into wine, a miracle attributed to Christ in Jn 2:1–11, and, in legends, to several other saints, including Adelm, Agnes, Aibert, Gerard, Gerluc the Penitent, Guido, Odilo, Peter the Hermit, Vaast, Victor of Plancy, and Zita. See Brewer, pp. 335–337. Baring-Gould describes the church built to commemorate the miracle (VIII: 627): 'The reputed house of Martha is now the church of S. Martha, a church with work of the twelfth century in it, but for the most part dating from the fourteenth. In the crypt beneath the nave, which is earlier, is the shrine and tomb of S. Martha, ornamented with her recumbent effigy in white marble, not badly executed, but modern. Against the walls the history of S. Martha is represented in a series of bas-reliefs in a sad state of mutilation. In the floor is a well, the water of which is said to rise and fall with the Rhône.' See also Vincent of Beauvais, *Speculum historiale*, p. 358.

2572. *Fronto.* The *South English Legendary* adds details about the relationship between Martha and Fronto not contained in VBMM and *Legenda aurea*. Fronto, according to SEL, was one of the seventy-two disciples of Christ and a close companion of the apostles. Brought up by Saint Martha, he regarded her has his nurse and mother, so when she lay ill, he came and confessed her and gave her the sacrament. See *The South English Legendary*, ed. Charlotte D'Evelyn and Anna J. Mill, 3 vols. (London: OUP, 1956–1959) I: 353, 130 ff.

2604–2606. *At last . . . longed.* From *Vita apostolica*

(Faillon, PL 112: 1502, note d.)

2610–2611. *'Come . . . throne.* As Kilian Walsh notes in his translation of Saint Bernard, Sermons on the Song of Songs, (CF 7: 82, n. 72), this phrase is from the response to the tenth lesson of the third nocturn of the common of virgins.

2618–2619. *eleventh kalends . . . glory.* From *Vita apostolica* (Faillon, PL 112: 1502, note e.) The eleventh kalends of August is July 22.

2619–2623. *Amidst the . . . . beauty.* The Virtues are one of the traditional nine orders of angels. Generally the Magdalen's seat in heaven is indicated in only the most general terms as 'among the heavenly choirs', but it is appropriate that VBMM place her with the Virtues, for, according to Saint Bernard, three activities for which Mary is noted — contemplation, miracle-working, and evangelization — are the special province of this angelic hierarchy: 'Other blessed spirits are named Virtues because their God-given vocation is to explore and admire with a happy curiosity the hidden and eternal causes of signs and wonders, signs that they display throughout the earth whenever they please by the powerful manipulation of the elements. As a consequence, these naturally burn with love for the Lord of Hosts, for Christ, the power of God. For it is an occupation full of sweetness and grace to contemplate the obscure mysteries of wisdom in Wisdom itself, a source of the greatest honor and glory that the effects produced by causes hidden in the Word of God should be revealed for the world's admiration by their ministry . . . God, therefore, is loved . . . by the Virtues for the overwhelming benignity revealed in his working of miracles by which he most aptly attracts unbelievers to the faith . . . (SC 19; CF 4.2, 6: 141, 144; SBOp 1: 109, 111).

2642. *most beautiful sister.* This epithet may be more than a casual compliment. The similar phrase, 'most beautiful of women', is commonly applied to the Virgin; to her antetype, the Bride in the Song of Songs; and to the Church. See, for example,

Gilbert of Hoyland, SC 47. 3, 4, 6 (CF 26: 562, 566; PL 184: 247, 249), and John of Ford, SC 2.3 (CF 29: 96; CCCM 17: 47–48). Gilbert applies the phrase 'most beautiful' to all souls possessing a spiritual grace, and especially to penitents: 'But many faithful and spiritual souls are also most beautiful, either because by their holy way of life they allow no stain or by careful and sincere confession they at once wash any stain away. Most beautiful in a way is one who, without surpassing all others, still does not transgress . . . Most beautiful then is the soul which dons splendor and confession, clothed in light as in a robe. Most beautiful is the soul which either is light itself or is clothed in light: by confession clothed in light, by its way of life existing as light itself.' (CF 26.3: 562; PL 184: 247.)

Saint Bernard compares the relative beauties of Mary and Martha by way of explicating the beauty of the Bride's cheeks. Spiritual beauty, says Bernard, is determined by two elements of 'intention' — matter and purpose, which are equivalent to deed and intent, or action and affection. These are the two cheeks of the bride. Those who possess only one of the two have a flawed or at most a lesser beauty. Active persons, represented by Martha, possess beauty of matter in good deeds, but because the active life inevitably draws one's attention away from God, they do not have complete beauty of purpose. Contemplatives, represented by Mary Magdalene, however, possess both beauties, since both their deeds and affections are rightly directed to God and to God alone: 'To give one's attention to something other than God, although for God's sake, means to embark on Martha's busy life rather than Mary's way of contemplation. I do not say that this soul is deformed, but it has not attained to perfect beauty . . . And therefore, to seek God for his own sake alone, this is to possess two cheeks made most beautiful by the two elements of intention.' (SC 40.3; CF 7: 200–201; SBOp 2: 25–26). Martha is beautiful but Mary is 'most beautiful'.

2715. *an image . . . Saviour.* I.e., a crucifix. Baring-Gould remarks: 'The cross of S. Martha, of copper, was preserved in the church at Tarascon till the Revolution, when it disappeared.' (VIII: 628.)

2733-2741. *story of . . . expired.* Jacobus, who does not identify the reader, says that the book was Luke's Gospel. See also Vincent of Beauvais, *Speculum historiale,* p. 359.

2742. *fourth kalends of August.* July 29.

2746-2747. *Her body . . . church.* In 1478, Louis XI of France provided a magnificent reliquary for Saint Martha's supposed remains at Tarascon. See *Acta Sanctorum,* July II: 19-20. And see *ibid.,* pp. 29-30 for an account by the notary Petrus Margoti and the magistrate Joannes Mutatoris, dated 13 August 1458, of relics and reliquaries at Tarascon and the care provided them by King René d'Anjou.

2764. *first kalends of August.* July 31.

2804-2807. *Finally, they . . . miracle.* 'The glove was preserved at Tarascon as a singular relic till the Revolution, when it disappeared.' Baring-Gould, VIII: 629.

2808-2812, *Some of . . . relates.* According to Jacobus, Marcella, surviving her mistress by ten years, journeyed into 'Sclavonia' where she preached and wrote a *vita* of Saint Martha. He is undoubtedly referring to the legend that the Bollandists cite as *Vita auct. pseudo-Marcilla interpretate pseudo-Suntyche'.* (BHL 5545-5546). Vincent of Beauvais, p. 361, also refers to this piece, which may indeed have been a common source for VBMM and *Speculum historiale.*

2816. *Saint Clement.* The 'fellow worker' of Paul the Apostle, mentioned in Ph 4: 3. Medieval legendaries frequently identify him with Pope Saint Clement, third or fourth bishop of Rome.

2822-2823. *Clovis, king . . . Teutons.* Clovis, or

Chlodovech, b. 465, r. 481–511. Founder of the merovingian dynasty, Clovis was baptized by Saint Remigius at Rheims. During his time, Septimania and Province were under the control of the Goths. The Franks did not conquor Province until 536.

2849–2874. *Seeing the . . . June.* From *Vita apostolica* (Faillon, PL 112: 1507–8, note c.)

2870–2871. Abbey of Saint Maximin. For the rivalry between Vézelay and Saint Maximin regarding the possession of Saint Mary Magdalene's relics, see Saxer, *Le culte* and *Le dossier,* and René Louis, *Girart, Comte, de Vienne, et ses fondations monastiques* (Auxerre: Bureaux de l'Imprimerie Moderne, 1946). The dispute was eventually resolved in favor of Saint Maximin, but in Saint Bernard's time, Vézelay enjoyed a grand pilgrimage cult devoted to the Magdalen.

# CISTERCIAN PUBLICATIONS, INC.
## TITLES LISTING

### —CISTERCIAN TEXTS—

#### BERNARD OF CLAIRVAUX

Apologia to Abbot William
Bernard of Clairvaux, Letters of
Five Books on Consideration: Advice to a Pope
Homilies in Praise of the Blessed Virgin Mary
Life and Death of Saint Malachy the Irishman
Love without Measure: Extracts from the
    Writings of St Bernard (Paul Dimier)
On Grace and Free Choice
On Loving God (Analysis by Emero Stiegman)
Parables and Sentences (Michael Casey)
Sermons for the Summer Season
Sermons on Conversion
Sermons on the Song of Songs I-IV
The Steps of Humility and Pride

#### WILLIAM OF SAINT THIERRY

The Enigma of Faith
Exposition on the Epistle to the Romans
Exposition on the Song of Songs
The Golden Epistle
The Mirror of Faith
The Nature and Dignity of Love
On Contemplating God: Prayer & Meditations

#### AELRED OF RIEVAULX

Dialogue on the Soul
Liturgical Sermons, I
Mirror of Charity
Spiritual Friendship
Treatises I: On Jesus at the Age of Twelve,
    Rule for a Recluse, The Pastoral Prayer
Walter Daniel: The Life of Aelred of Rievaulx

#### JOHN OF FORD

Sermons on the Final Verses of the
    Songs of Songs I-VII

#### GILBERT OF HOYLAND

Sermons on the Songs of Songs I-III
Treatises, Sermons and Epistles

#### OTHER EARLY
#### CISTERCIAN WRITERS

Adam of Perseigne, Letters of
Alan of Lille: The Art of Preaching
Amadeus of Lausanne: Homilies in Praise of
    Blessed Mary
Baldwin of Ford: Spiritual Tractates I-II
Gertrud the Great: Spiritual Exercises
Gertrud the Great: The Herald of God's
    Loving-Kindness
Guerric of Igny: Liturgical Sermons I-[II]
Helinand of Froidmont: Verses on Death

Idung of Prüfening: Cistercians and Cluniacs:
    The Case for Cîteaux
Isaac of Stella: Sermons on the Christian Year,
    I-[II]
The Life of Beatrice of Nazareth
Serlo of Wilton & Serlo of Savigny: Seven
    Unpublished Works
Stephen of Lexington: Letters from Ireland
Stephen of Sawley: Treatises

### —MONASTIC TEXTS—

#### EASTERN CHRISTIAN TRADITION

Besa: The Life of Shenoute
Cyril of Scythopolis: Lives of the Monks of
    Palestine
Dorotheos of Gaza: Discourses and Sayings
Evagrius Ponticus: Praktikos and Chapters on
    Prayer
Handmaids of the Lord: Lives of Holy Women
    in Late Antiquity & Early Middle Ages
    (Joan Petersen)
Harlots of the Desert (Benedicta Ward)
John Moschos: The Spiritual Meadow
Lives of the Desert Fathers
Lives of Simeon Stylites (Robert Doran)
Luminous Eye (Sebastian Brock)
Mena of Nikiou: Isaac of Alexandra & St
    Macrobius
Pachomian Koinonia I-III (Armand Veilleux)
Paphnutius: Histories/Monks of Upper Egypt
Sayings of the Desert Fathers
    (Benedicta Ward)
Spiritual Direction in the Early Christian East
    (Irénée Hausherr)
Spiritually Beneficial Tales of Paul, Bishop of
    Monembasia (John Wortley)
Symeon the New Theologian: The Theological
    and Practical Treatises & The Three
    Theological Discourses (Paul McGuckin)
Theodoret of Cyrrhus: A History of the
    Monks of Syria
The Syriac Fathers on Prayer and the Spiritual
    Life (Sebastian Brock)

#### WESTERN CHRISTIAN
#### TRADITION

Anselm of Canterbury: Letters I-III
    (Walter Fröhlich)
Bede: Commentary...Acts of the Apostles
Bede: Commentary...Seven Catholic Epistles
Bede: Homilies on the Gospels III
The Celtic Monk (U. Ó Maidín)
Gregory the Great: Forty Gospel Homilies
Life of the Jura Fathers
Maxims of Stephen of Muret

# CISTERCIAN PUBLICATIONS, INC.
## TITLES LISTING

Meditations of Guigo I, Prior of the
    Charterhouse (A. Gordon Mursall)
Peter of Celle: Selected Works
Letters of Rancé I–II
Rule of the Master
Rule of Saint Augustine
Wound of Love: A Carthusian Miscellany

### CHRISTIAN SPIRITUALITY

Cloud of Witnesses: The Development of
    Christian Doctrine (David N. Bell)
Call of Wild Geese (Matthew Kelty)
Cistercian Way (André Louf)
The Contemplative Path
Drinking From the Hidden Fountain
    (Thomas Špidlík)
Eros and Allegory: Medieval Exegesis of the
    Song of Songs (Denys Turner)
Fathers Talking (Aelred Squire)
Friendship and Community (Brian McGuire)
From Cloister to Classroom
Life of St Mary Magdalene and of Her Sister
    St Martha (David Mycoff)
Many Mansions (David N. Bell)
Mercy in Weakness (André Louf)
Name of Jesus (Irénée Hausherr)
No Moment Too Small (Norvene Vest)
Penthos: The Doctrine of Compunction in the
    Christian East (Irénée Hausherr)
Rancé and the Trappist Legacy
    (A.J. Krailsheimer)
Russian Mystics (Sergius Bolshakoff)
Sermons in a Monastery (Matthew Kelty)
Silent Herald of Unity: The Life of
    Maria Gabrielle Sagheddu (Martha
    Driscoll)
Spirituality of the Christian East
    (Thomas Špidlík)
Spirituality of the Medieval West
    (André Vauchez)
Tuning In To Grace (André Louf)
Wholly Animals: A Book of Beastly Tales
    (David N. Bell)

### —MONASTIC STUDIES—

Community and Abbot in the Rule of
    St Benedict I–II (Adalbert de Vogüé)
Finances of the Cistercian Order in the
    Fourteenth Century (Peter King)
Fountains Abbey and Its Benefactors
    (Joan Wardrop)
The Hermit Monks of Grandmont
    (Carole A. Hutchison)
In the Unity of the Holy Spirit
    (Sighard Kleiner)
Joy of Learning & the Love of God:
    Essays in Honor of Jean Leclercq
Monastic Odyssey (Marie Kervingant)

Monastic Practices (Charles Cummings)
Occupation of Celtic Sites in Ireland
    (Geraldine Carville)
Reading St Benedict (Adalbert de Vogüé)
Rule of St Benedict: A Doctrinal and Spiritual
    Commentary (Adalbert de Vogüé)
Rule of St Benedict (Br. Pinocchio)
St Hugh of Lincoln (David H. Farmer)
Stones Laid Before the Lord (Anselme Dimier)
Venerable Bede (Benedicta Ward)
What Nuns Read (David N. Bell)
With Greater Liberty: A Short History of
    Christian Monasticism & Religious
    Orders (Karl Frank)

### —CISTERCIAN STUDIES—

Aelred of Rievaulx: A Study (Aelred Squire)
Athirst for God: Spiritual Desire in Bernard of
    Clairvaux's Sermons on the Song of
    Songs (Michael Casey)
Beatrice of Nazareth in Her Context
    (Roger De Ganck)
Bernard of Clairvaux: Man, Monk, Mystic
    (Michael Casey) [tapes and readings]
Bernardus Magister (Nonacentenary)
Catalogue of Manuscripts in the Obrecht
    Collection of the Institute of Cistercian
    Studies (Anna Kirkwood)
Christ the Way: The Christology of Guerric of
    Igny (John Morson)
Cistercian Abbeys of Britain
Cistercians in Denmark (Brian McGuire)
Cistercians in Medieval Art (James France)
Cistercians in Scandinavia (James France)
A Difficult Saint (Brian McGuire)
Dore Abbey (Shoesmith & Richardson)
A Gathering of Friends: Learning & Spirituality
    in John of Forde (Costello and
    Holdsworth)
Image and Likeness: The Augustinian
    Spirituality of William of St Thierry
    (David Bell)
Index of Authors & Works in Cistercian
    Libraries in Great Britain I (David Bell)
Index of Cistercian Authors and Works in
    Medieval Library Catalogues in Great
    Britian (David Bell)
Mystical Theology of St Bernard
    (Étienne Gilson)
The New Monastery: Texts & Studies on the
    Earliest Cistercians
Nicolas Cotheret's Annals of Cîteaux
    (Louis J. Lekai)
Pater Bernhardus (Franz Posset)
A Second Look at Saint Bernard
    (Jean Leclercq)
The Spiritual Teachings of St Bernard of
    Clairvaux (John R. Sommerfeldt)

# CISTERCIAN PUBLICATIONS, INC.

## TITLES LISTING

Studies in Medieval Cistercian History (various)
Studiosorum Speculum (Louis J. Lekai)
Three Founders of Cîteaux
   (Jean-Baptiste Van Damme)
Towards Unification with God (Beatrice of
   Nazareth in Her Context, 2)
William, Abbot of St Thierry
Women and St Bernard of Clairvaux
   (Jean Leclercq)

### MEDIEVAL RELIGIOUS
### —WOMEN—

*Lillian Thomas Shank and John A. Nichols, editors*
Distant Echoes
Hidden Springs: Cistercian Monastic Women
   (2 volumes)
Peace Weavers

### —CARTHUSIAN—
### TRADITION

Call of Silent Love (A Carthusian)
Freedom of Obedience (A Carthusian)
Guigo II: The Ladder of Monks & Twelve
   Meditations (Colledge & Walsh)
Interior Prayer (A Carthusian)
Meditations of Guigo II (A. Gordon Mursall)
Prayer of Love and Silence (A Carthusian)
Way of Silent Love (A Carthusian Miscellany)
Wound of Love (A Carthusian Miscellany)
They Speak by Silences (A Carthusian)
Where Silence is Praise (A Carthusian)

### -STUDIES IN CISTERCIAN-
### ART & ARCHITECTURE

*Meredith Parsons Lillich, editor*
Volumes II-V are now available

### —THOMAS MERTON—

Climate of Monastic Prayer (T. Merton)
Legacy of Thomas Merton (P. Hart)
Message of Thomas Merton (P. Hart)
Monastic Journey of Thomas Merton (P. Hart)
Thomas Merton/Monk (P. Hart)
Thomas Merton on St Bernard
Toward an Integrated Humanity
   (M. Basil Pennington, ed.)

### CISTERCIAN LITURGICAL
### —DOCUMENTS SERIES—

*Chrysogonus Waddell, ocso, editor*
Hymn Collection of the...Paraclete
*Institutiones nostrae:* The Paraclete Statutes
Molesme Summer-Season Breviary (4 volumes)
Old French Ordinary & Breviary of the Abbey
   of the Paraclete (2 volumes)

Twelfth-century Cistercian Hymnal
   (2 volumes)
The Twelfth-century Cistercian Psalter
Two Early Cistercian *Libelli Missarum*

### -STUDIA PATRISTICA XVIII-

#### Volumes 1, 2 and 3

❖ ❖ ❖ ❖ ❖ ❖ ❖ ❖ ❖ ❖ ❖ ❖ ❖ ❖

Editorial queries & advance book
information should be directed to the
Editorial Offices:

Cistercian Publications
1201 Oliver Street
Western Michigan University
Kalamazoo, Michigan 49008
Tel: (616) 387-8920 • Fax: (616) 387-8921

. . .

Customers may order
these books through booksellers
or directly by contacting the warehouse
at the address below:

Cistercian Publications
Saint Joseph's Abbey
167 North Spencer Road
Spencer, Massachusetts 01562-1233
Tel: (508) 885-8730 • Fax: (508) 885-4687
email: cistpub@spencerabbey.org

. . .

**Canadian Orders:**
Novalis
49 Front Street East, Second Floor
Toronto, Ontario M5E 1B3
Telephone: 416-363-3303 1-800-387-7164
Fax: 416-363-9409

. . .

**British & European Orders:**
Cistercian Publications
Mount Saint Bernard Abbey
Coalville, Leicester LE67 5UL
Fax: [44] (1530) 81.46.08

. . .

*Cistercian Publications is a non-profit
corporation. Its publishing program is
restricted to monastic texts in translation
and books on the monastic tradition.*

*A complete catalogue of texts in
translation and studies on early,
medieval, and modern monasticism is
available, free of charge, by contacting
any of the addresses above.*

Saint Gregory Nazianzen: Selected Poems

Eight Chapters on Perfection and Angel's Song
(Walter Hilton)

Creative Suffering (Iulia de Beausobre)

Bringing Forth Christ. Five Feasts of the Child
Jesus (St Bonaventure)

Gentleness in St John of the Cross

*Distributed in North America only for Fairacres Press.*

### DISTRIBUTED BOOKS

St Benedict: Man with An Idea (Melbourne Studies)

The Spirit of Simplicity

Benedict's Disciples (David Hugh Farmer)

The Emperor's Monk: A Contemporary Life of
Benedict of Aniane

A Guide to Cistercian Scholarship (2nd ed.)

*North American customers may order
through booksellers or directly from
the publisher:*

    Cistercian Publications
    St Joseph's Abbey
    Spencer, Massachusetts  01562
    (508) 885–7011

    Cistercian Publications
    Editorial Offices
    WMU Station
    Kalamazoo, Michigan  49008
    (616) 387–5090

*A complete catalogue of texts-in-
translation and studies on early,
medieval, and modern Christian
monasticism is available at no
cost from Cistercian Publications.*

*Cistercian monks and nuns have been
living lives of prayer & praise, meditation
& manual labor since the twelfth century.
They are part of an unbroken tradition
which extends back to the fourth century
and which continues today in the Catholic
church, the Orthodox churches, the
Anglican communion, and most recently,
in the Protestant churches.*

*Share their way of life and their search for
God by reading Cistercian Publications.*